HIGHER

# RELIGIOUS, MORAL & PHILOSOPHICAL STUDIES
## Specimen Question Paper
## 2010-2013

| | |
|---|---|
| Hodder Gibson Study Skills Advice – General | – page 3 |
| Hodder Gibson Study Skills Advice – Higher Religious, Moral & Philosophical Studies | – page 5 |
| SPECIMEN QUESTION PAPER | – page 7 |
| 2010 EXAM | – page 25 |
| 2011 EXAM | – page 43 |
| 2012 EXAM | – page 61 |
| 2013 EXAM | – page 79 |
| ANSWER SECTION | – page 97 |

SQA

HODDER
GIBSON
LEARN MORE

Hodder Gibson is grateful to the copyright holders, as credited on the final page of the Question Section, for permission to use their material. Every effort has been made to trace the copyright holders and to obtain their permission for the use of copyright material. Hodder Gibson will be happy to receive information allowing us to rectify any error or omission in future editions.

Hachette UK's policy is to use papers that are natural, renewable and recyclable products and made from wood grown in sustainable forests. The logging and manufacturing processes are expected to conform to the environmental regulations of the country of origin.

Orders: please contact Bookpoint Ltd, 130 Park Drive, Abingdon, Oxon OX14 4SE. Telephone: (44) 01235 827720. Fax: (44) 01235 400454.

Lines are open 9.00–5.00, Monday to Saturday, with a 24-hour message answering service. Visit our website at www.hoddereducation.co.uk. Hodder Gibson can be contacted direct on: Tel: 0141 848 1609; Fax: 0141 889 6315; email: hoddergibson@hodder.co.uk

This collection first published in 2013 by

Hodder Gibson, an imprint of Hodder Education,

An Hachette UK Company

2a Christie Street

Paisley PA1 1NB

{BrightRED   Hodder Gibson is grateful to Bright Red Publishing Ltd for collaborative work in preparation of this book and all
PUBLISHING   SQA Past Paper and National 5 Model Paper titles 2013.

Typeset by PDQ Digital Media Solutions Ltd, Bungay, Suffolk NR35 1BY

Printed in the UK

A catalogue record for this title is available from the British Library

ISBN 978-1-4718-0301-7

3 2 1

2014 2013

# Introduction

## Study Skills – what you need to know to pass exams!

### Pause for thought

Many students might skip quickly through a page like this. After all, we all know how to revise. Do you really though?

### Think about this:

"IF YOU ALWAYS DO WHAT YOU ALWAYS DO, YOU WILL ALWAYS GET WHAT YOU HAVE ALWAYS GOT."

Do you like the grades you get? Do you want to do better? If you get full marks in your assessment, then that's great! Change nothing! This section is just to help you get that little bit better than you already are.

There are two main parts to the advice on offer here. The first part highlights fairly obvious things but which are also very important. The second part makes suggestions about revision that you might not have thought about but which WILL help you.

### Part 1

DOH! It's so obvious but …

### Start revising in good time

Don't leave it until the last minute – this will make you panic.

Make a revision timetable that sets out work time AND play time.

### Sleep and eat!

Obvious really, and very helpful. Avoid arguments or stressful things too – even games that wind you up. You need to be fit, awake and focused!

### Know your place!

Make sure you know exactly **WHEN and WHERE** your exams are.

### Know your enemy!

**Make sure you know what to expect in the exam.**

How is the paper structured?

How much time is there for each question?

What types of question are involved?

Which topics seem to come up time and time again?

Which topics are your strongest and which are your weakest?

Are all topics compulsory or are there choices?

### Learn by DOING!

There is no substitute for past papers and practice papers – they are simply essential! Tackling this collection of papers and answers is exactly the right thing to be doing as your exams approach.

### Part 2

People learn in different ways. Some like low light, some bright. Some like early morning, some like evening / night. Some prefer warm, some prefer cold. But everyone uses their BRAIN and the brain works when it is active. Passive learning – sitting gazing at notes – is the most INEFFICIENT way to learn anything. Below you will find tips and ideas for making your revision more effective and maybe even more enjoyable. What follows gets your brain active, and active learning works!

### Activity 1 – Stop and review

#### Step 1

When you have done no more than 5 minutes of revision reading STOP!

#### Step 2

Write a heading in your own words which sums up the topic you have been revising.

#### Step 3

Write a summary of what you have revised in no more than two sentences. Don't fool yourself by saying, 'I know it but I cannot put it into words'. That just means you don't know it well enough. If you cannot write your summary, revise that section again, knowing that you must write a summary at the end of it. Many of you will have notebooks full of blue/black ink writing. Many of the pages will not be especially attractive or memorable so try to liven them up a bit with colour as you are reviewing and rewriting. **This is a great memory aid, and memory is the most important thing.**

## Activity 2 — Use technology!

Why should everything be written down? Have you thought about 'mental' maps, diagrams, cartoons and colour to help you learn? And rather than write down notes, why not record your revision material?

What about having a text message revision session with friends? Keep in touch with them to find out how and what they are revising and share ideas and questions.

Why not make a video diary where you tell the camera what you are doing, what you think you have learned and what you still have to do? No one has to see or hear it but the process of having to organise your thoughts in a formal way to explain something is a very important learning practice.

Be sure to make use of electronic files. You could begin to summarise your class notes. Your typing might be slow but it will get faster and the typed notes will be easier to read than the scribbles in your class notes. Try to add different fonts and colours to make your work stand out. You can easily Google relevant pictures, cartoons and diagrams which you can copy and paste to make your work more attractive and **MEMORABLE**.

## Activity 3 – This is it. Do this and you will know lots!

### Step 1

In this task you must be very honest with yourself! Find the SQA syllabus for your subject (www.sqa.org.uk). Look at how it is broken down into main topics called MANDATORY knowledge. That means stuff you MUST know.

### Step 2

BEFORE you do ANY revision on this topic, write a list of everything that you already know about the subject. It might be quite a long list but you only need to write it once. It shows you all the information that is already in your long-term memory so you know what parts you do not need to revise!

### Step 3

Pick a chapter or section from your book or revision notes. Choose a fairly large section or a whole chapter to get the most out of this activity.

With a buddy, use Skype, Facetime, Twitter or any other communication you have, to play the game "If this is the answer, what is the question?". For example, if you are revising Geography and the answer you provide is "meander", your buddy would have to make up a question like "What is the word that describes a feature of a river where it flows slowly and bends often from side to side?".

Make up 10 "answers" based on the content of the chapter or section you are using. Give this to your buddy to solve while you solve theirs.

### Step 4

Construct a wordsearch of at least 10 X 10 squares. You can make it as big as you like but keep it realistic. Work together with a group of friends. Many apps allow you to make wordsearch puzzles online. The words and phrases can go in any direction and phrases can be split. Your puzzle must only contain facts linked to the topic you are revising. Your task is to find 10 bits of information to hide in your puzzle but you must not repeat information that you used in Step 3. DO NOT show where the words are. Fill up empty squares with random letters. Remember to keep a note of where your answers are hidden but do not show your friends. When you have a complete puzzle, exchange it with a friend to solve each other's puzzle.

### Step 5

Now make up 10 questions (not "answers" this time) based on the same chapter used in the previous two tasks. Again, you must find NEW information that you have not yet used. Now it's getting hard to find that new information! Again, give your questions to a friend to answer.

### Step 6

As you have been doing the puzzles, your brain has been actively searching for new information. Now write a NEW LIST that contains only the new information you have discovered when doing the puzzles. Your new list is the one to look at repeatedly for short bursts over the next few days. Try to remember more and more of it without looking at it. After a few days, you should be able to add words from your second list to your first list as you increase the information in your long-term memory.

## FINALLY! Be inspired...

Make a list of different revision ideas and beside each one write **THINGS I HAVE** tried, **THINGS I WILL** try and **THINGS I MIGHT** try. Don't be scared of trying something new.

And remember – "FAIL TO PREPARE AND PREPARE TO FAIL!"

# Higher Religious, Moral & Philosophical Studies

## The course

The first thing you will notice about Higher RMPS is that it differs greatly from 'core' RME – with regards to content, skills utilised and expectations. In order to be successful in Higher RMPS, you will need to be highly focused and committed. While the subject is very demanding, it offers you the opportunity to study, in depth, a world religion which many of you will know little about, as well as encouraging you to analyse and evaluate arguments surrounding morality, contemporary ethical issues and issues of belief and science. Higher RMPS comprises of three sections:

1. World Religion
2. Morality in the Modern World
3. Belief and Science.

### How the course is graded

The grade you finally achieve for Higher RMPS depends on two things:

- The internal assessments you do in school or college (the "NABs") – these don't count towards the final grade, but you must have passed them before you can achieve a final grade.

- The external exam you sit in May/June – that's what this book is all about!

### The exam

The exam is split into two papers:

- Paper 1 – Morality in the Modern World and Christianity: Belief & Science
- Paper 2 – World Religion.

Paper 1 lasts 1 hour 55 minutes, and is worth 80 marks. Paper 2 lasts 55 minutes and is worth 40 marks.

The SQA gives detailed advice in the Candidate Guidance Information section of the Higher RMPS page on its website: http://www.sqa.org.uk/sqa/40982.html.

## Tackling the questions

Probably the most important thing to remember while you're answering the questions is to pay attention to the number of **marks** and the **code**. Doing this won't give you all the right answers, admittedly, but it should prevent you from making a lot of the common errors. The questions are split into KU (Knowledge and Understanding) and AE (Analysis and Evaluation). The KU questions generally require you to focus on the 'what' – giving general descriptions of areas you have studied – whereas the AE questions are more focused on the 'why' and the 'how'. Answers to the AE questions will generally require more depth, and will often require you to consider different viewpoints.

There are **three** questions in each section – broken into (a), (b), (c), etc – and you will generally be asked to answer one or two KU questions before answering an AE question. This format allows you to build up a picture of what you know before considering your (or another's) viewpoint.

## Tackling the KU questions

While it is acceptable to make short statements in a KU question and still gain full marks, be careful that you follow the instruction given in the question. A 'Describe...' question must include a description. For example:

2010 Christianity: Belief & Science Question (a)
Describe how scientific method gives us knowledge about the nature of reality. **(4KU)**

> Science uses observation, hypothesis, experimentation and verification to understand the nature of reality.

This answer would gain **no marks**. While factually correct, the question asks for a description. Markers would expect something more like this from a Higher candidate:

> Science uses observation hypothesis, experimentation and verification to understand the nature of reality. To begin with, a scientist will look at something in nature and then after that he will make some kind of statement about how the thing in nature works. He will then devise an experiment to see if he is right in his statement or hypothesis and once he has done the experiment he will make his results available to other scientists who can check to see if the knowledge he has given is right.

This answer would gain **four marks**. The candidate has given a brief explanation of what each aspect means as a short paragraph. However, a KU answer can also include a bullet point list:

- Observation (you observe something in nature).
- Hypothesis (you make a statement about it).
- Experimentation (you do experiments to test your hypothesis).
- Verification (you get the results checked by your peers).

Here, the candidate has clearly stated each process and followed this up with a (very) brief description. This answer would gain four marks.

## Tackling the AE questions and the final question

It is often helpful to begin an AE answer with a point of KU. Provided that this is relevant, and has not been mentioned previously, the KU point can gain a mark and it will act as a 'settler' for you. An AE question will often focus on responses to a statement or issue. It is important to establish which response(s) you are being asked to analyse – your own, religious or non-religious (secular). Remember, it is not enough just to make a statement about the issue or quotation (*"**Some** Christians, for example Roman Catholics, would completely disagree with the statement"*). You must explain **why**. It is worth noting at this point that sources, which are generally very underused, can enhance the quality of an AE answer and can help you to gain more marks (*"**Some** Christians, for example Roman Catholics, would completely disagree with the statement due to the fact that it contradicts Jesus' teaching of 'Love thy neighbour'"*). It is also worth noting that when asked for religious responses you should (a) identify which religion you are referring to and (b) ensure that you do not imply that **all** Christians/Jews/Sikhs/etc hold the same views.

Ensure that you read the final question carefully before you begin to attempt an answer. It is worth going back to previous exam papers and having a look at the wording used to set up questions. For example, questions that ask you "What extent..." or "How far do you agree..." are looking for treatment of both sides of the issue. Whereas questions such as "Explain why you/religious people/non-religious people disagree" or "Explain how this view can be justified" are only looking for a one-sided treatment. Similarly, when faced with a statement/quotation, make sure you read it carefully to establish which "side" it is on before you begin to construct your answer.

## Good luck!

Remember that the rewards for passing Higher RMPS are well worth it! In the exam, be confident in your own ability. If you're not sure how to answer a question, trust your instincts and just give it a go anyway. Keep calm and don't panic! GOOD LUCK!

Please be aware that the format of the
Higher exam changed in 2010 and we
have only included the papers in this
book that are relevant to the new course.

**HIGHER | 2013 Specimen Question Paper**

[BLANK PAGE]

**[RMPS/SQP336]**

# Religious, Moral and Philosophical Studies
## Higher

Time: 1 hours 45 mins

# NATIONAL QUALIFICATIONS

Paper 1
Specimen Question Paper
for use in and after 2010

**There are two Sections in this paper:**
Section 1 – Morality in the Modern World
Section 2 – Christianity: Belief and Science

Section 1: You should only answer the question on the topic you have studied.

Topic 1 – Crime and Punishment **or**
Topic 2 – Gender **or**
Topic 3 – Global Issues **or**
Topic 4 – Medical Ethics **or**
Topic 5 – War and Peace

Section 2: All questions are mandatory.

The skills of knowledge and understanding (KU) and analysis and evaluation (AE) are being assessed in this paper. When answering each question you should note the number of marks allocated to each skill as indicated after each part of the question.

**SECTION 1**

*Marks   Code*

**Morality in the Modern World**

**Topic 1 – Crime and Punishment**

**Reminder:** *You should answer these questions if you have studied* **Crime and Punishment** *in the Morality in the Modern World Unit.*

**Instructions:** Answer **all** the questions. The marks available for each question are indicated. You should use this as a guide to the amount of detail you should include in your answer.

1. (*a*) Describe the Euthyphro dilemma.    **3   KU**

   (*b*) What is the role of sacred writings in religious morality?    **4   KU**

   (*c*) Explain the main features of utilitarian ethics.    **3   KU**

   (*d*) How might utilitarians respond to issues arising from capital punishment?    **4   AE**

2. (*a*) Describe **two** sentences that might be given to criminals in UK courts.    **4   KU**

   (*b*) Explain **two** drawbacks of punishing criminals.    **8   AE**

3. (*a*) Using at least one example, describe how the causes of crime have been addressed.    **6   KU**

   (*b*) Why might addressing the causes of crime be a matter of importance for religious people?    **8   AE**

   **(40)**

## Topic 2 – Gender Issues

*Marks Code*

**Reminder:** *You should answer these questions if you have studied **Gender Issues** in the Morality in the Modern World Unit.*

**Instructions:** Answer **all** questions. The marks available for each question are indicated. You should use these as a guide to the amount of detail you should include in your answer.

1.  (*a*)  Describe the Euthyphro dilemma. — **3 KU**

    (*b*)  What is the role of sacred writings in religious morality? — **4 KU**

    (*c*)  Explain the main features of utilitarian ethics. — **3 KU**

    (*d*)  How might utilitarians respond to issues arising from gender roles in the UK? — **4 AE**

2.  (*a*)  Describe **two** ways in which the media stereotypes women. — **4 KU**

    (*b*)  Explain **two** drawbacks of media stereotyping of women. — **8 AE**

3.  (*a*)  Using at least one example, describe ways in which women in the developing world have suffered violence. — **6 KU**

    (*b*)  Why might violence against women be a matter of importance for religious people? — **8 AE**

                                                                                **(40)**

## Topic 3 – Global Issues

*Marks*  *Code*

**Reminder:** *You should answer these questions if you have studied **Global Issues** in the Morality in the Modern World Unit.*

**Instructions:** Answer **all** questions. The marks available for each question are indicated. You should use this as a guide to the amount of detail you should include in your answer.

1. (*a*) Describe the Euthyphro dilemma. — **3 KU**

   (*b*) What is the role of sacred writings in religious morality? — **4 KU**

   (*c*) Explain the main features of utilitarian ethics. — **3 KU**

   (*d*) How might utilitarians respond to issues arising from globalisation? — **4 AE**

2. (*a*) Describe **two** causes of global warming. — **4 KU**

   (*b*) Explain **two** dangers of global warming. — **8 AE**

3. (*a*) Using at least one example, describe what is meant by "globalisation". — **6 KU**

   (*b*) Why might globalisation be a matter of importance for religious people? — **8 AE**

**(40)**

## Topic 4 – Medical Ethics

*Marks Code*

**Reminder:** *You should answer these questions if you have studied **Medical Ethics** in the Morality in the Modern World Unit.*

**Instructions:** Answer **all** questions. The marks available for each question are indicated. You should use this as a guide to the amount of detail you should include in your answer.

1. (*a*) Describe the Euthyphro dilemma.     **3**   **KU**

    (*b*) What is the role of sacred writings in religious morality?     **4**   **KU**

    (*c*) Explain the main features of utilitarian ethics.     **3**   **KU**

    (*d*) How might utilitarians respond to the moral implications of euthanasia?     **4**   **AE**

2. (*a*) Describe **two** circumstances in which IVF might be used.     **4**   **KU**

    (*b*) Explain **two** drawbacks of IVF.     **8**   **AE**

3. (*a*) Using at least one example, describe what is meant by "voluntary euthanasia".     **6**   **KU**

    (*b*) Why might voluntary euthanasia be a matter of importance for religious people?     **8**   **AE**

                                                **(40)**

## Topic 5 – War and Peace

*Marks   Code*

**Reminder:** *You should answer these questions if you have studied **War and Peace** in the Morality in the Modern World Unit.*

**Instructions:** Answer **all** questions. The marks available for each question are indicated. You should use this as a guide to the amount of detail you should include in your answer.

1. (a)  Describe the Euthyphro dilemma.                                            **3**   **KU**

   (b)  What is the role of sacred writings in religious morality?                  **4**   **KU**

   (c)  Explain the main features of utilitarian ethics.                            **3**   **KU**

   (d)  How might utilitarians respond to issues arising from responses to war?     **4**   **AE**

2. (a)  Describe **two** causes of war.                                            **4**   **KU**

   (b)  Explain **two** drawbacks of going to war.                                 **8**   **AE**

3. (a)  Using at least one example, describe what is meant by "weapons of mass destruction".   **6**   **KU**

   (b)  Why might the use of weapons of mass destruction be a matter of importance for religious people?   **8**   **AE**

                                                                                   **(40)**

*[END OF SECTION 1]*

## SECTION 2

*Marks   Code*

### Christianity: Belief and Science

**Instructions:** Answer **all** questions. The marks available for each question are indicated. You should use these as a guide to the amount of detail you should include in your answer.

1.  (*a*)  Describe **two** types of revelation.    **4**  **KU**

    (*b*)  What is scientific method?    **4**  **KU**

    (*c*)  Explain **two** differences between the scientific method and revelation.    **6**  **AE**

2.  (*a*)  What supporting evidence do scientists offer for the Big Bang Theory?    **4**  **KU**

    (*b*)  According to Genesis, how did the universe come into existence?    **4**  **KU**

    (*c*)  *"Some Christians accept the Big Bang Theory while others reject the whole idea."*

        Explain why there is disagreement amongst Christians on this issue.    **6**  **AE**

3.  (*a*)  Describe the key features of the Teleological Argument.    **6**  **KU**

    (*b*)  Explain **two** strengths and **two** weaknesses of the Teleological Argument.    **8**  **AE**

                                                  **(40)**

*[END OF SECTION 2]*

*[END OF SPECIMEN QUESTION PAPER]*

[BLANK PAGE]

**[RMPS/SQP336]**

# Religious, Moral and Philosophical Studies Higher

Time: 55 mins

# NATIONAL QUALIFICATIONS

Paper 2
Specimen Question Paper
for use in and after 2010

You should answer **either**

Section 1:     Buddhism

**or**

Section 2:     Christianity

**or**

Section 3:     Hinduism

**or**

Section 4:     Islam

**or**

Section 5:     Judaism

**or**

Section 6:     Sikhism

The skills of knowledge and understanding (KU) and analysis and evaluation (AE) are being assessed in this paper. When answering each question you should note the number of marks allocated to each skill as indicated after each part of the question.

## Section 1 – Buddhism

*Marks  Code*

**Reminder:** *You should choose this section if you have studied **Buddhism** in the World Religion Unit.*

**Instructions:** *Answer **all** questions. The marks available for each question are indicated. Use these as a guide to the amount of detail you should include in your answer.*

1.  (*a*)  What are the Three Root Poisons?                                                      3    KU

    (*b*)  Explain **three** effects of the Root Poisons.                                         6    AE


2.  (*a*)  What do Buddhists believe about samsara?                                             6    KU

    (*b*)  In what ways do Buddhists understand Nibbana?                                         3    KU

    (*c*)  "*Aiming for a better Samsaric existence would be a more realistic aim than aiming for Nibbana.*"

           Would all Buddhists agree with this statement?                                        6    AE


3.  (*a*)  Describe the Buddhist idea of the arhat.                                              4    KU

    (*b*)  What is bodhisattva?                                                                  4    KU

    (*c*)  "*An arhat is the only true Buddhist.*"

           How might Buddhists respond to this statement?                                        8    AE

                                                                                               (40)

## Section 2 – Christianity

*Marks    Code*

**Reminder:** *You should choose this section if you have studied **Christianity** in the World Religion Unit.*

**Instructions:** *Answer **all** questions. The marks available for each question are indicated. Use these as a guide to the amount of detail you should include in your answer.*

1. (*a*)  What relationship do Christians believe God has with human beings?                     **3**    **KU**

   (*b*)  Explain **three** effects of God's relationship with human beings.                         **6**    **AE**

2. (*a*)  What do the parables of Jesus teach about living the Christian life?                       **6**    **KU**

   (*b*)  In what ways do Christians describe Heaven?                                                 **3**    **KU**

   (*c*)  *"Eternal life can only be gained by living a Christian life."*

   Would all Christians agree with this statement?                                                    **6**    **AE**

3. (*a*)  Describe what Christians mean by "sacraments".                                              **4**    **KU**

   (*b*)  In what ways do Christians fight social injustice?                                          **4**    **KU**

   (*c*)  *"Fighting social injustice is more important than participating in the sacraments."*

   How might Christians respond to this statement?                                                    **8**    **AE**

                                                                                                     **(40)**

**Section 3 – Hinduism**                                             *Marks   Code*

**Reminder:**  *You should choose this section if you have studied **Hinduism** in the World Religion Unit.*

**Instructions:**  *Answer **all** questions.  The marks available for each question are indicated.  Use these as a guide to the amount of detail you should include in your answer.*

1.  (*a*)  What do Hindus understand by the term "The Three Gunas"?          3    **KU**

    (*b*)  Explain **three** effects of the gunas.                           6    **AE**

2.  (*a*)  What do Hindus teach about the atman?                             6    **KU**

    (*b*)  In what ways do Hindus describe moksha?                           3    **KU**

    (*c*)  *"Achieving moksha is beyond most ordinary Hindus."*

            Would all Hindus agree with this statement?                      6    **AE**

3.  (*a*)  Describe what Hindus mean by the margas.                          4    **KU**

    (*b*)  What is dharma?                                                    4    **KU**

    (*c*)  *"The margas are not nearly as important as dharma in the Hindu quest for moksha."*

            How might Hindus respond to this statement?                      8    **AE**

                                                                            **(40)**

**Section 4 – Islam**    *Marks  Code*

**Reminder:** *You should choose this section if you have studied* **Islam** *in the World Religion Unit.*

**Instructions:** *Answer* **all** *questions. The marks available for each question are indicated. Use these as a guide to the amount of detail you should include in your answer.*

1. (*a*) What do muslims understand by the term "freewill"?    3    **KU**

   (*b*) Explain **three** effects of the misuse of freewill.    6    **AE**

2. (*a*) What do Muslims teach about submission?    6    **KU**

   (*b*) In what ways do Muslims describe Akhirah?    3    **KU**

   (*c*) *"Faithfulness to Allah is all that is required to gain eternal life."*
   Would all Muslims agree with this statement?    6    **AE**

3. (*a*) Describe how Muslims prepare for salah.    4    **KU**

   (*b*) What do Muslims consider to be the purpose of salah?    4    **KU**

   (*c*) *"Salah benefits only the individual."*
   How might Muslims respond to this statement?    8    **AE**

   **(40)**

## Section 5 – Judaism

*Marks*  *Code*

**Reminder:**  *You should choose this section if you have studied **Judaism** in the World Religion Unit.*

**Instructions:**  *Answer **all** questions.  The marks available for each question are indicated.  Use these as a guide to the amount of detail you should include in your answer.*

1. (*a*)  What do Jews understand by God's will?  3  **KU**

   (*b*)  Explain **three** effects of ignoring God's will.  6  **AE**

2. (*a*)  What do Jews teach about "the world to come"?  6  **KU**

   (*b*)  Describe Jewish beliefs about the Messianic Age.  3  **KU**

   (*c*)  *"Belief in the Messianic Age is more important than belief in the world to come."*

   Would all Jews agree with this statement?  6  **AE**

3. (*a*)  Describe the importance of the Oral Traditions.  4  **KU**

   (*b*)  In what ways is the Torah used in Judaism?  4  **KU**

   (*c*)  *"Without the oral traditions, the Torah would be meaningless."*

   How might Jews respond to this statement?  8  **AE**

   (40)

## Section 6 – Sikhism

*Marks*   *Code*

**Reminder:** *You should choose this section if you have studied **Sikhism** in the World Religion Unit.*

**Instructions:** *Answer **all** questions. The marks available for each question are indicated. Use these as a guide to the amount of detail you should include in your answer.*

1. (a) What do Sikhs understand by the phrase "separation from God"?    **3**   **KU**

   (b) Explain **three** effects of separation from God.    **6**   **AE**

2. (a) In what ways do Sikhs try to live a God-centred life?    **6**   **KU**

   (b) What do Sikhs understand by the phrase "reunion with God"?    **3**   **KU**

   (c) *"Living a good life is more realistic than achieving reunion with God."*
   Would all Sikhs agree with this statement?    **6**   **AE**

3. (a) Describe the importance of Guru Nanak.    **4**   **KU**

   (b) In what ways is respect shown to the Guru Granth Sahib?    **4**   **KU**

   (c) *"Guru Nanak was the First Guru and is therefore the most important for Sikhs."*
   How might Sikhs respond to this statement?    **8**   **AE**

   **(40)**

*[END OF SPECIMEN QUESTION PAPER]*

[BLANK PAGE]

**HIGHER**

# 2010

[BLANK PAGE]

# X265/301

| | | |
|---|---|---|
| NATIONAL QUALIFICATIONS 2010 | MONDAY, 31 MAY 1.00 PM – 2.45 PM | RELIGIOUS, MORAL AND PHILOSOPHICAL STUDIES HIGHER Paper 1 |

**There are two Sections in this paper:**

Section 1 – Morality in the Modern World
Section 2 – Christianity: Belief and Science

Section 1: You should only answer the question on the topic you have studied.

Question 1 – Gender **or**
Question 2 – Crime and Punishment **or**
Question 3 – Global Issues **or**
Question 4 – Medical Ethics **or**
Question 5 – War and Peace.

Section 2 has **one** mandatory question.

The skills of knowledge and understanding (KU) and analysis and evaluation (AE) are being assessed in this paper. When answering each question you should note the number of marks allocated to each skill as indicated after each part of the question.

*Marks Code*

## SECTION 1

### Morality in the Modern World

### Question 1 – Gender

**Reminder:** *You should answer this question if you have studied **Gender Issues** in the Morality in the Modern World Unit.*

**Instructions:** Answer **all** parts of the question *(a)* – *(i)*. The number of marks available for each part of the question is indicated. You should use these as a guide to the amount of detail you should include in your answer.

|   |   |   |   |
|---|---|---|---|
| (a) | What is religious morality based upon? | 4 | KU |
| (b) | Describe Utilitarian ethics. | 3 | KU |
| (c) | Describe **two** gender issues affecting the UK today. | 4 | KU |
| (d) | In the UK, what is meant by "equal opportunities"? | 2 | KU |
| (e) | Explain **two** religious concerns about current gender issues in the UK. | 6 | AE |
| (f) | Describe **two** international responses to issues affecting women in the developing world. | 4 | KU |
| (g) | "International responses to issues affecting women in the developing world can bring benefits." Do you agree with this statement? | 6 | AE |
| (h) | Describe the main features of Kantian ethics. | 3 | KU |
| (i) | In what ways might Kantian ethics be applied to issues arising from the treatment of women in the developing world? | 8 | AE |

**(40)**

## Question 2 – Crime and Punishment                                    *Marks   Code*

**Reminder:** *You should answer this question if you have studied Crime and Punishment in the Morality in the Modern World Unit.*

**Instructions:** Answer **all** parts of the question **(a) – (i)**. The number of marks available for each part of the question is indicated. You should use these as a guide to the amount of detail you should include in your answer.

(*a*) What is religious morality based upon?                              4    **KU**

(*b*) Describe Utilitarian ethics.                                       3    **KU**

(*c*) Describe **two** causes of crime.                                  4    **KU**

(*d*) What does reform aim to achieve?                                   2    **KU**

(*e*) Explain **two** religious concerns about crime.                    6    **AE**

(*f*) Describe **two** methods of execution.                             4    **KU**

(*g*) "The death penalty can bring benefits to society."

   Do you agree with this statement?                                     6    **AE**

(*h*) Describe the main features of Kantian ethics.                      3    **KU**

(*i*) In what ways might Kantian ethics be applied to issues arising from capital punishment?                                                8    **AE**

                                                                    (40)

                                                              **[Turn over**

## Question 3 – Global Issues

*Marks　Code*

**Reminder:** *You should answer this question if you have studied **Global Issues** in the Morality in the Modern World Unit.*

**Instructions:** Answer **all** parts of the question **(a) – (i)**. The number of marks available for each part of the question is indicated. You should use these as a guide to the amount of detail you should include in your answer.

| | | |
|---|---:|:--|
| (a) What is religious morality based upon? | 4 | KU |
| (b) Describe Utilitarian ethics. | 3 | KU |
| (c) Describe **two** causes of poverty. | 4 | KU |
| (d) In what ways can the poor in the developing world be supported? | 2 | KU |
| (e) Explain **two** religious concerns about poverty. | 6 | AE |
| (f) Give **two** examples of international responses to global warming. | 4 | KU |
| (g) "International responses to global warming can bring benefits to the world."<br><br>Do you agree with this statement? | 6 | AE |
| (h) Describe the main features of Kantian ethics. | 3 | KU |
| (i) In what ways might Kantian ethics be applied to issues arising from global warming? | 8 | AE |

**(40)**

### Question 4 – Medical Ethics                    *Marks   Code*

**Reminder:** *You should answer this question if you have studied **Medical Ethics** in the Morality in the Modern World Unit.*

**Instructions:** Answer **all** parts of the question **(a) – (i)**. The number of marks available for each part of the question is indicated. You should use these as a guide to the amount of detail you should include in your answer.

(a)  What is religious morality based upon?                    4   KU

(b)  Describe Utilitarian ethics.                    3   KU

(c)  Describe **two** uses of embryos.                    4   KU

(d)  In what ways does UK law regulate the use of embryos?                    2   KU

(e)  Explain **two** religious concerns about the use of embryos.                    6   AE

(f)  Describe **two** situations in which non-voluntary euthanasia might be considered.                    4   KU

(g)  "Non-voluntary euthanasia can bring benefits to society."

Do you agree with this statement?                    6   AE

(h)  Describe the main features of Kantian ethics.                    3   KU

(i)  In what ways might Kantian ethics be applied to issues arising from euthanasia?                    8   AE

                    (40)

**[Turn over**

## Question 5 – War and Peace

*Marks*　*Code*

**Reminder:** *You should answer this question if you have studied **War and Peace** in the Morality in the Modern World Unit.*

**Instructions:** Answer **all** parts of the question **(a) – (i)**. The number of marks available for each part of the question is indicated. You should use these as a guide to the amount of detail you should include in your answer.

(a) What is religious morality based upon?　　　　4　KU

(b) Describe Utilitarian ethics.　　　　3　KU

(c) Describe **two** reasons for declaring war.　　　　4　KU

(d) In what ways might an individual be pacifist?　　　　2　KU

(e) Explain **two** religious concerns about the reasons for declaring war.　　　　6　AE

(f) Give **two** examples of the damage nuclear weapons can cause.　　　　4　KU

(g) "Nuclear weapons can bring benefits to the world".

　　Do you agree with this statement?　　　　6　AE

(h) Describe the main features of Kantian ethics.　　　　3　KU

(i) In what ways might Kantian ethics be applied to issues arising from modern armaments?　　　　8　AE

**(40)**

*[END OF SECTION 1]*

**SECTION 2**                                                                    *Marks   Code*

**Christianity:  Belief and Science**

**Instructions:**  Answer **all** parts of the question **(a) – (h)**.  The number of marks available for each part of the question is indicated.  You should use these as a guide to the amount of detail you should include in your answer.

(*a*)  Describe how scientific method gives us knowledge about the nature of reality.                                                                              **4    KU**

(*b*)  Describe what is meant by revelation in the Christian tradition.              **4    KU**

(*c*)  "Scientific method is no more reliable than revelation".

How far would Christians agree with this statement?                          **6    AE**

(*d*)  In what ways does the cosmological argument answer the questions about the origins of the universe?                                                         **4    KU**

(*e*)  Explain **two** criticisms of the cosmological argument.                      **4    AE**

(*f*)   In what ways do Christians describe the origin of human life?                **4    KU**

(*g*)  Describe how science explains the origins of human life.                      **4    KU**

(*h*)  "God is the best explanation for the origin of human life."

To what extent can this claim be justified?                                 **10    AE**

**(40)**

*[END OF SECTION 2]*

*[END OF QUESTION PAPER]*

[BLANK PAGE]

# X265/302

| | | |
|---|---|---|
| NATIONAL QUALIFICATIONS 2010 | MONDAY, 31 MAY 3.05 PM – 4.00 PM | RELIGIOUS, MORAL AND PHILOSOPHICAL STUDIES HIGHER Paper 2 |

You should answer **either**

Section 1:    Buddhism

**or**

Section 2:    Christianity

**or**

Section 3:    Hinduism

**or**

Section 4:    Islam

**or**

Section 5:    Judaism

**or**

Section 6:    Sikhism

The skills of knowledge and understanding (KU) and analysis and evaluation (AE) are being assessed in this paper. When answering each question you should note the number of marks allocated to each skill as indicated after each part of the question.

## Section 1 – Buddhism

*Marks    Code*

**Reminder:** *You should choose this section if you have studied* **Buddhism** *in the World Religion Unit.*

## Question

**Instructions:** Answer **all** parts of the question **(a)–(g)**. The number of marks available for each part of the question is indicated. You should use these as a guide to the amount of detail you should include in your answer.

(*a*)  Describe what Buddhists understand by Dukkha.                                    4    **KU**

(*b*)  Explain the relationship between Dukkha and other aspects of the human condition.                                                                            4    **AE**

(*c*)  What is the Sangha?                                                              4    **KU**

(*d*)  "The Sangha benefits only monks and nuns, not the laity."

Do you agree?                                                                     8    **AE**

(*e*)  What are the main moral principles of Buddhism?                                   6    **KU**

(*f*)  In what ways do Buddhists meditate?                                              6    **KU**

(*g*)  "Living a moral life is more important than meditating."

Explain at least **two** ways in which Buddhists might respond to this statement.                                                                         8    **AE**

**(40)**

## Section 2 – Christianity

*Marks   Code*

**Reminder:** *You should choose this section if you have studied **Christianity** in the World Religion Unit.*

**Question**

**Instructions:** Answer **all** parts of the question **(a)–(g)**. The number of marks available for each part of the question is indicated. You should use these as a guide to the amount of detail you should include in your answer.

(a)  Describe what Christians understand by the term "sin".                                4    **KU**

(b)  Explain the relationship between sin and other aspects of the human condition.                                                                                                      4    **AE**

(c)  Describe the events surrounding the resurrection of Jesus.                              4    **KU**

(d)  "Belief in the resurrection alone is not enough to lead a Christian life."

Do you agree?                                                                                           8    **AE**

(e)  What do Christians understand by prayer?                                                    6    **KU**

(f)  In what ways do Christians put their faith into action?                                  6    **KU**

(g)  "Action is more important than prayer."

Explain at least **two** ways in which Christians might respond to this statement.                                                                                                  8    **AE**

(40)

**[Turn over**

**Section 3 – Hinduism**    *Marks   Code*

**Reminder:** *You should choose this section if you have studied* **Hinduism** *in the World Religion Unit.*

**Question**

**Instructions:** Answer **all** parts of the question **(a)–(g)**. The number of marks available for each part of the question is indicated. You should use these as a guide to the amount of detail you should include in your answer.

| | | |
|---|---|---|
| (*a*) Describe what Hindus understand by transience. | **4** | **KU** |
| (*b*) Explain the relationship between transience and other aspects of the human condition. | **4** | **AE** |
| (*c*) Describe Karma Marga. | **4** | **KU** |
| (*d*) "Karma Marga brings few benefits to society."<br>Do you agree? | **8** | **AE** |
| (*e*) What do Hindus understand by moksha? | **6** | **KU** |
| (*f*) What do Hindus understand by the jiva? | **6** | **KU** |
| (*g*) "The jiva does not attain moksha. It dies with the body."<br>Explain at least **two** ways in which Hindus might respond to this statement. | **8**<br>**(40)** | **AE** |

**Section 4 – Islam**                    *Marks   Code*

**Reminder:** *You should choose this section if you have studied **Islam** in the World Religion Unit.*

**Question**

**Instructions:** Answer **all** parts of the question **(a)–(g)**. The number of marks available for each part of the question is indicated. You should use these as a guide to the amount of detail you should include in your answer.

(a)  Describe what Muslims understand by suffering.                                    **4   KU**

(b)  Explain the relationship between suffering and other aspects of the human condition.                                                                                     **4   AE**

(c)  Describe Zakat.                                                                    **4   KU**

(d)  "Zakat brings more benefit to the community than the individual Muslim."

Do you agree?                                                                          **8   AE**

(e)  What are the goals of life for Muslims?                                            **6   KU**

(f)  What obstacles might there be to achieving these goals during life?                **6   KU**

(g)  "The most significant belief for Muslims is the Day of Judgement."

Explain at least **two** ways in which Muslims might respond to this statement.          **8   AE**
                                                                                       **(40)**

**[Turn over**

## Section 5 – Judaism

Marks　Code

**Reminder:** *You should choose this section if you have studied **Judaism** in the World Religion Unit.*

**Question**

**Instructions:** Answer **all** parts of the question **(a)–(g)**. The number of marks available for each part of the question is indicated. You should use these as a guide to the amount of detail you should include in your answer.

(a) Describe what Jews understand by freewill.　　4　**KU**

(b) Explain the relationship between freewill and other aspects of the human condition.　　4　**AE**

(c) Describe Jewish beliefs about the Torah.　　4　**KU**

(d) "Observing the laws of the Torah is impossible to do."

Do you agree?　　8　**AE**

(e) What are the goals of life for Jews?　　6　**KU**

(f) What are the obstacles to achieving these goals of life?　　6　**KU**

(g) "All that the Jewish goals of life have achieved for Jews is suffering."

Explain at least **two** ways in which Jews might respond to this statement.　　8　**AE**

(40)

**Section 6 – Sikhism**                                          *Marks   Code*

**Reminder:**  *You should choose this section if you have studied **Sikhism** in the World Religion Unit.*

**Question**

**Instructions:**  Answer **all** parts of the question **(a)–(g)**.  The number of marks available for each part of the question is indicated.  You should use these as a guide to the amount of detail you should include in your answer.

(*a*)  Describe what Sikhs understand by the term Hukam.                    **4    KU**

(*b*)  Explain how Hukam is related to other aspects of the human condition in Sikhism.                                                          **4    AE**

(*c*)  Describe the sangat.                                              **4    KU**

(*d*)  "Being part of the sangat alone is not enough to be a true Sikh."

      Do you agree?                                                       **8    AE**

(*e*)  What do Sikhs understand by Jivan mukti?                          **6    KU**

(*f*)  In what ways do Sikhs practice Sewa and Simran in their lives?    **6    KU**

(*g*)  "Sewa achieves more for the individual and society than Simran."

      Explain at least **two** ways in which Sikhs might respond to this statement.    **8    AE**
                                                                              **(40)**

*[END OF QUESTION PAPER]*

[BLANK PAGE]

HIGHER

2011

[BLANK PAGE]

# X265/301

| | | |
|---|---|---|
| NATIONAL QUALIFICATIONS 2011 | MONDAY, 30 MAY 1.00 PM – 2.45 PM | RELIGIOUS, MORAL AND PHILOSOPHICAL STUDIES HIGHER Paper 1 |

**There are two Sections in this paper:**
Section 1 – Morality in the Modern World
Section 2 – Christianity:  Belief and Science

Section 1:  You should only answer the question on the topic you have studied.

Topic 1 – Crime and Punishment **or**
Topic 2 – Gender **or**
Topic 3 – Global Issues **or**
Topic 4 – Medical Ethics **or**
Topic 5 – War and Peace.

Section 2: All questions are mandatory.

The skills of knowledge and understanding (KU) and analysis and evaluation (AE) are being assessed in this paper.  When answering each question you should note the number of marks allocated to each skill as indicated after each part of the question.

**SECTION 1**

*Marks Code*

**Morality in the Modern World**

**Topic 1 – Crime and Punishment**

**Reminder:** *You should answer this question if you have studied **Crime and Punishment** in the Morality in the Modern World Unit.*

**Instructions:** Answer **all** the questions. The marks available for each question are indicated. You should use these as a guide to the amount of detail you should include in your answer.

1. (a) To what issue does the Euthyphro Dilemma refer? **4 KU**

   (b) In Kantian Ethics, what is the Categorical Imperative? **3 KU**

   (c) Give a description of the sources of religious morality. **3 KU**

   (d) Evaluate a religious viewpoint you have studied on the purposes of punishment. **4 AE**

2. (a) Describe one case of an individual who has been sentenced to death. **3 KU**

   (b) Describe UN Declarations that are relevant to Capital Punishment. **3 KU**

   (c) "Regardless of what the UN says, any nation should have the right to take the lives of murderers."

   Explain **two** reasons why some people disagree with this statement. **6 AE**

3. (a) Describe what community service involves. **4 KU**

   (b) "Society will never improve if offenders are given sentences such as community service."

   Evaluate **at least one** secular viewpoint on this statement. **10 AE**

   **(40)**

## Topic 2 – Gender

*Marks   Code*

**Reminder:** *You should answer this question if you have studied* **Gender** *in the Morality in the Modern World Unit.*

**Instructions:** Answer **all** the questions. The marks available for each question are indicated. You should use these as a guide to the amount of detail you should include in your answer.

1. (a)   To what issue does the Euthyphro Dilemma refer?                                    4    **KU**

   (b)   In Kantian Ethics, what is the Categorical Imperative?                             3    **KU**

   (c)   Give a description of the sources of religious morality.                           3    **KU**

   (d)   Evaluate a religious viewpoint you have studied on gender issues in the
         UK.                                                                               4    **AE**


2. (a)   What causes poor health in women in the developing world?                          3    **KU**

   (b)   Describe the situation regarding the education of females in the
         developing world.                                                                 3    **KU**

   (c)   "Education is the main barrier to equality for women in the developing
         world."

         Explain **two** reasons why some people disagree with this statement.             6    **AE**


3. (a)   Describe the changing role of women in the workplace in the UK.                    4    **KU**

   (b)   "Traditionally, men have gone out to work and women have had a more
         domestic role—this benefits UK society."

         Evaluate **at least one** secular viewpoint on this statement.                    10    **AE**

                                                                                          (40)


**[Turn over**

## Topic 3 – Global Issues

*Marks* *Code*

**Reminder:** *You should answer this question if you have studied **Global Issues** in the Morality in the Modern World Unit.*

**Instructions:** Answer **all** the questions. The marks available for each question are indicated. You should use these as a guide to the amount of detail you should include in your answer.

1.   (*a*)   To what issue does the Euthyphro Dilemma refer?      4   KU

    (*b*)   In Kantian Ethics, what is the Categorical Imperative?      3   KU

    (*c*)   Give a description of the sources of religious morality.      3   KU

    (*d*)   Evaluate a religious viewpoint you have studied on the global distribution of wealth and resources.      4   AE

2.   (*a*)   Describe the causes of global warming.      3   KU

    (*b*)   Describe international responses to the problem of global warming.      3   KU

    (*c*)   "Responses to the problem of global warming are 'too little too late'."

        Explain **two** reasons why some people disagree with this statement.      6   AE

3.   (*a*)   Describe what is meant by globalisation.      4   KU

    (*b*)   "Globalisation benefits the rich more than it does the poor."

        Evaluate **at least one** secular viewpoint on this statement.      10   AE

                                          **(40)**

## Topic 4 – Medical Ethics

*Marks　Code*

**Reminder:** *You should answer this question if you have studied **Medical Ethics** in the Morality in the Modern World Unit.*

**Instructions:** Answer **all** the questions. The marks available for each question are indicated. You should use these as a guide to the amount of detail you should include in your answer.

1. (*a*)　To what issue does the Euthyphro Dilemma refer?　　　　**4　KU**

　(*b*)　In Kantian Ethics, what is the Categorical Imperative?　　　**3　KU**

　(*c*)　Give a description of the sources of religious morality.　　　**3　KU**

　(*d*)　Evaluate a religious viewpoint you have studied on the use of embryos.　**4　AE**

2. (*a*)　Describe the UK laws regarding voluntary euthanasia.　　　**3　KU**

　(*b*)　Describe the Netherlands' law on voluntary euthanasia.　　**3　KU**

　(*c*)　"Euthanasia laws provide adequate protection for everyone involved in it."

　　　Explain **two** reasons why some people disagree with this statement.　**6　AE**

3. (*a*)　What reasons might there be for selecting a human embryo?　**4　KU**

　(*b*)　"Embryo selection is morally right in all cases."

　　　Evaluate **at least one** secular viewpoint on this statement.　**10　AE**

　　　　　　　　　　　　　　　　　　　　**(40)**

**[Turn over**

## Topic 5 – War and Peace    *Marks   Code*

**Reminder:** *You should answer this question if you have studied **War and Peace** in the Morality in the Modern World Unit.*

**Instructions:** Answer **all** the questions. The marks available for each question are indicated. You should use these as a guide to the amount of detail you should include in your answer.

1. (a)  To what issue does the Euthyphro Dilemma refer?    **4   KU**

   (b)  In Kantian Ethics, what is the Categorical Imperative?    **3   KU**

   (c)  Give a description of the sources of religious morality.    **3   KU**

   (d)  Evaluate a religious viewpoint you have studied on different responses to war.    **4   AE**

2. (a)  Describe what makes a weapon "conventional".    **3   KU**

   (b)  What is meant by "weapons of mass destruction"?    **3   KU**

   (c)  "The possession of weapons of mass destruction is the best way to maintain peace."

   Explain **two** reasons why some people disagree with this statement.    **6   AE**

3. (a)  What forms might conscientious objection take?    **4   KU**

   (b)  "Conscientious objection cannot be right when faced with aggression."

   Evaluate **at least one** secular viewpoint on this statement.    **10   AE**

    **(40)**

*[END OF SECTION 1]*

**SECTION 2**                                                    *Marks*   *Code*

**Christianity: Belief and Science**

**Instructions:** Answer **all** the questions. The marks available for each question are indicated. You should use these as a guide to the amount of detail you should include in your answer.

1.  (a)   Describe the Teleological Argument for the existence of God.                                    4     **KU**

    (b)   What evidence from nature is used to support this argument?                                     4     **KU**

    (c)   Explain how evidence from nature might be used to challenge the
          Teleological Argument.                                                                          6     **AE**


2.  (a)   Describe the Cosmological Argument.                                                             4     **KU**

    (b)   To what extent is the Big Bang Theory compatible with the
          Cosmological Argument?                                                                          4     **AE**


3.  (a)   What method is used by scientists to investigate the world around us?                           4     **KU**

    (b)   In what ways do Christians believe God reveals himself to human
          beings?                                                                                         4     **KU**

    (c)   "The main difference between scientific method and revelation is that
          science is able to prove what it claims."

          To what extent do you agree with this statement?                                               10    **AE**

                                                                                                       **(40)**


*[END OF SECTION 2]*


*[END OF QUESTION PAPER]*

[BLANK PAGE]

# X265/302

| NATIONAL QUALIFICATIONS 2011 | MONDAY, 30 MAY 3.05 PM – 4.00 PM | RELIGIOUS, MORAL AND PHILOSOPHICAL STUDIES HIGHER Paper 2 |

You should answer **either**

Section 1:     Buddhism

**or**

Section 2:     Christianity

**or**

Section 3:     Hinduism

**or**

Section 4:     Islam

**or**

Section 5:     Judaism

**or**

Section 6:     Sikhism

The skills of knowledge and understanding (KU) and analysis and evaluation (AE) are being assessed in this paper. When answering each question you should note the number of marks allocated to each skill as indicated after each part of the question.

### Section 1 – Buddhism

*Marks* *Code*

**Reminder:** *You should choose this section if you have studied* **Buddhism** *in the World Religion Unit.*

**Instructions:** Answer **all** the questions. The marks available for each question are indicated. Use these as a guide to the amount of detail you should include in your answer.

1. (*a*) How do Buddhists describe the human condition?      6   KU

   (*b*) "Anicca is central to Buddhist understanding of the human condition."

   To what extent do you agree?      6   AE

2. (*a*) What do Buddhists mean by Nibbana?      6   KU

   (*b*) Explain the impact of belief in Nibbana on the lives of Buddhists.      6   AE

3. (*a*) Describe **two** of the Five Precepts.      4   KU

   (*b*) Describe ways in which Buddhists show devotion to the Buddha.      4   KU

   (*c*) "There is no more important practice than devotion to the Buddha."

   How far would Buddhists agree with this statement?      8   AE

   **(40)**

**Section 2 – Christianity**                               *Marks   Code*

**Reminder:** *You should choose this section if you have studied* **Christianity** *in the World Religion Unit.*

**Instructions:** Answer **all** the questions. The marks available for each question are indicated. Use these as a guide to the amount of detail you should include in your answer.

1. (*a*) How do Christians describe the human condition?                      6    **KU**

   (*b*) "Human disobedience is central to Christian understanding of the human condition."

   To what extent do you agree?                                              6    **AE**


2. (*a*) In what ways do Christians understand Judgement?                     6    **KU**

   (*b*) Explain the impact of belief in Judgement on the lives of Christians. 6    **AE**


3. (*a*) Describe how Christians celebrate communion.                         4    **KU**

   (*b*) In what ways do Christians perform baptisms?                         4    **KU**

   (*c*) "There is no practice more important than baptism."

   How far would Christians agree with this statement?                       8    **AE**

                                                                            (40)


**[Turn over**

**Section 3 – Hinduism**    *Marks    Code*

**Reminder:** *You should choose this section if you have studied* **Hinduism** *in the World Religion Unit.*

**Instructions:** Answer **all** the questions. The marks available for each question are indicated. Use these as a guide to the amount of detail you should include in your answer.

1.  (*a*)  How do Hindus describe the human condition?    6    **KU**

    (*b*)  "Samsara is central to Hindu understanding of the human condition."

    To what extent do you agree?    6    **AE**


2.  (*a*)  In what ways do Hindus describe kama and artha?    6    **KU**

    (*b*)  Explain the impact of kama and artha on the lives of Hindus.    6    **AE**


3.  (*a*)  Describe how Hindus follow bhakti marga.    4    **KU**

    (*b*)  Give a description of jnana marga.    4    **KU**

    (*c*)  "There is no marga more important than jnana."

    How far would Hindus agree with this statement?    8    **AE**

    **(40)**

## Section 4 – Islam

*Marks   Code*

**Reminder:** *You should choose this section if you have studied **Islam** in the World Religion Unit.*

**Instructions:** Answer **all** the questions. The marks available for each question are indicated. Use these as a guide to the amount of detail you should include in your answer.

1. (*a*) How do Muslims describe the human condition?                                      6    **KU**

   (*b*) "The concept of freewill is central to Muslim understanding of the human condition."

   To what extent do you agree?                                                            6    **AE**

2. (*a*) What do Muslims understand by the term Resurrection?                              6    **KU**

   (*b*) Explain the impact of believing in Resurrection on the lives of Muslims.         6    **AE**

3. (*a*) What are the rules associated with Sawm?                                         4    **KU**

   (*b*) Describe the main events of Hajj.                                                4    **KU**

   (*c*) "There is no pillar more important than Hajj."

   How far would Muslims agree with this statement?                                       8    **AE**

                                                                                        **(40)**

**[Turn over**

**Section 5 – Judaism**                                                     *Marks    Code*

**Reminder:** *You should choose this section if you have studied **Judaism** in the World Religion Unit.*

**Instructions:** Answer **all** the questions. The marks available for each question are indicated. Use these as a guide to the amount of detail you should include in your answer.

1. (*a*)  How do Jews describe the human condition?                          6    **KU**

   (*b*)  "The concept of freewill is central to Jewish understanding of the human condition."

   To what extent do you agree?                                             6    **AE**


2. (*a*)  Describe Jewish understandings of the Messianic Age.                6    **KU**

   (*b*)  Explain the impact of belief in the Messianic Age on the lives of Jews.   6    **AE**


3. (*a*)  Describe how Jews observe Kashrut.                                  4    **KU**

   (*b*)  What do Jews do on Shabbat?                                         4    **KU**

   (*c*)  "There is no religious duty more important than observing Shabbat."

   How far would Jews agree with this statement?                            8    **AE**

                                                                          **(40)**

**Section 6 – Sikhism**                                                      *Marks   Code*

**Reminder:** *You should choose this section if you have studied* **Sikhism** *in the World Religion Unit.*

**Instructions:** Answer **all** the questions. The marks available for each question are indicated. Use these as a guide to the amount of detail you should include in your answer.

1. (*a*) How do Sikhs describe the human condition?                          6   **KU**

   (*b*) "Maya is central to Sikh understanding of the human condition."

      To what extent do you agree?                                           6   **AE**


2. (*a*) Sikhs believe that there are Five Evils. Describe **three** of the Five Evils that must be avoided.                                                6   **KU**

   (*b*) Explain the impact of belief in the Five Evils on the lives of Sikhs.   6   **AE**


3. (*a*) Describe Nam Japna.                                                  4   **KU**

   (*b*) How do Sikhs carry out Vand Chhakna?                                 4   **KU**

   (*c*) "There is no religious duty more important than Vand Chhakna."

      How far would Sikhs agree with this statement?                         8   **AE**

                                                                            (40)

*[END OF QUESTION PAPER]*

[BLANK PAGE]

HIGHER

# 2012

[BLANK PAGE]

# X265/12/01

| NATIONAL QUALIFICATIONS 2012 | TUESDAY, 29 MAY 1.00 PM – 2.45 PM | RELIGIOUS, MORAL AND PHILOSOPHICAL STUDIES HIGHER Paper 1 |
|---|---|---|

**There are two Sections in this paper:**

Section 1 – Morality in the Modern World

Section 2 – Christianity:  Belief and Science

Section 1:  You should only answer all the questions on the topic you have studied.

Topic 1 – Crime and Punishment **or**

Topic 2 – Gender **or**

Topic 3 – Global Issues **or**

Topic 4 – Medical Ethics **or**

Topic 5 – War and Peace.

Section 2:  All questions are mandatory.

The skills of knowledge and understanding (KU) and analysis and evaluation (AE) are being assessed in this paper.  When answering each question you should note the number of marks allocated to each skill as indicated after each part of the question.

## SECTION 1

*Marks   Code*

### Morality in the Modern World

### Topic 1 – Crime and Punishment

**Reminder:** *Topic 1 is for candidates who have studied **Crime and Punishment** in the Morality in the Modern World Unit.*

**Instructions:** Answer **all** the questions. The marks available for each question are indicated. You should use these as a guide to the amount of detail you should include in your answer.

1.    (*a*)   What issues concerning morality does the Euthyphro Dilemma raise?    **4   KU**

     (*b*)   What are the key principles of Utilitarian Ethics?    **4   KU**

     (*c*)   Describe **two** purposes of punishment.    **4   KU**

     (*d*)   Explain Utilitarian views on the purpose of punishment.    **4   AE**

2.    (*a*)   Describe what is meant by "economic causes of crime".    **4   KU**

     (*b*)   "Economic causes of crime raise many moral concerns."

         Explain **two** of these concerns.    **6   AE**

3.    (*a*)   Describe religious teaching on the death penalty.    **4   KU**

     (*b*)   "A religious person should never support the death penalty."

         How far do you agree?    **10   AE**

                                                     **(40)**

## Topic 2 – Gender

*Marks  Code*

**Reminder:** *Topic 2 is for candidates who have studied* **Gender** *in the Morality in the Modern World Unit.*

**Instructions:** Answer **all** the questions. The marks available for each question are indicated. You should use these as a guide to the amount of detail you should include in your answer.

1. (*a*) What issues concerning morality does the Euthyphro Dilemma raise? **4 KU**

   (*b*) What are the key principles of Utilitarian Ethics? **4 KU**

   (*c*) Describe **two** gender issues in the United Kingdom. **4 KU**

   (*d*) Explain Utilitarian views on gender issues affecting men and women in the United Kingdom. **4 AE**

2. (*a*) Describe what is meant by the trafficking of females. **4 KU**

   (*b*) "The trafficking of females raises many moral concerns."

   Explain **two** of these concerns. **6 AE**

3. (*a*) Describe religious teaching on the empowerment of women. **4 KU**

   (*b*) "A religious person should always support the empowerment of women."

   How far do you agree? **10 AE**

   **(40)**

**[Turn over**

## Topic 3 – Global Issues

*Marks    Code*

**Reminder:**    *Topic 3 is for candidates who have studied **Global Issues** in the Morality in the Modern World Unit.*

**Instructions:**    Answer **all** the questions.   The marks available for each question are indicated.   You should use these as a guide to the amount of detail you should include in your answer.

1.  (*a*)  What issues concerning morality does the Euthyphro Dilemma raise?    **4    KU**

    (*b*)  What are the key principles of Utilitarian Ethics?    **4    KU**

    (*c*)  Describe **two** causes of global warming.    **4    KU**

    (*d*)  Explain Utilitarian views on global warming.    **4    AE**

2.  (*a*)  Describe what is meant by "stewardship of the environment".    **4    KU**

    (*b*)  "Poor stewardship of the environment raises many moral concerns."

    Explain **two** of these concerns.    **6    AE**

3.  (*a*)  Describe religious teaching on the distribution of the world's wealth and resources.    **4    KU**

    (*b*)  "A religious person should always support a fairer distribution of the world's wealth and resources."

    How far do you agree?    **10    AE**

    **(40)**

## Topic 4 – Medical Ethics

*Marks Code*

**Reminder:** *Topic 4 is for candidates who have studied* **Medical Ethics** *in the Morality in the Modern World Unit.*

**Instructions:** Answer **all** the questions. The marks available for each question are indicated. You should use these as a guide to the amount of detail you should include in your answer.

1. (*a*) What issues concerning morality does the Euthyphro Dilemma raise? 4 **KU**

   (*b*) What are the key principles of Utilitarian Ethics? 4 **KU**

   (*c*) Describe **two** uses of human embryos. 4 **KU**

   (*d*) Explain Utilitarian views on the uses of human embryos. 4 **AE**

2. (*a*) Describe what is meant by "voluntary euthanasia". 4 **KU**

   (*b*) "Voluntary euthanasia raises many moral concerns."

   Explain **two** of these concerns. 6 **AE**

3. (*a*) Describe religious teaching on the status of the embryo. 4 **KU**

   (*b*) "A religious person should never support interference with human embryos."

   How far do you agree? 10 **AE**

   (40)

**[Turn over**

## Topic 5 – War and Peace

*Marks    Code*

**Reminder:** *Topic 5 is for candidates who have studied **War and Peace** in the Morality in the Modern World Unit.*

**Instructions:** Answer **all** the questions. The marks available for each question are indicated. You should use these as a guide to the amount of detail you should include in your answer.

1. (a) What issues concerning morality does the Euthyphro Dilemma raise?    4  **KU**

   (b) What are the key principles of Utilitarian Ethics?    4  **KU**

   (c) Give **two** reasons why a country would declare war.    4  **KU**

   (d) Explain Utilitarian views on the morality of war.    4  **AE**


2. (a) What is understood by the term "biological weapons"?    4  **KU**

   (b) "Biological weapons raise many moral concerns."

   Explain **two** of these concerns.    6  **AE**


3. (a) Describe religious teaching on the morality of war.    4  **KU**

   (b) "A religious person should never fight in a war."

   How far do you agree?    10  **AE**

   **(40)**


*[END OF SECTION 1]*

**SECTION 2**

*Marks    Code*

**Christianity: Belief and Science**

**Reminder:** *This section should be answered by all candidates.*

**Instructions:** Answer **all** the questions. The marks available for each question are indicated. You should use these as a guide to the amount of detail you should include in your answer.

1. (*a*) What is meant by "revelation" in the Christian tradition?    **6    KU**

   (*b*) Why do some people consider Christian revelation to be limited?    **4    AE**

2. (*a*) Describe the Cosmological Argument.    **6    KU**

   (*b*) "There is no contradiction between the Cosmological Argument and scientific explanations for the origins of the universe."

   How far do you agree?    **6    AE**

3. (*a*) Describe the process of evolution.    **5    KU**

   (*b*) How does Genesis chapter 2 describe the creation of human beings?    **3    KU**

   (*c*) "It is possible to accept evolution and to believe that God created human life."

   How far would Christians agree with this statement?    **10    AE**

   **(40)**

*[END OF SECTION 2]*

*[END OF QUESTION PAPER]*

[BLANK PAGE]

# X265/12/02

| | | |
|---|---|---|
| NATIONAL QUALIFICATIONS 2012 | TUESDAY, 29 MAY 3.05 PM – 4.00 PM | RELIGIOUS, MORAL AND PHILOSOPHICAL STUDIES HIGHER Paper 2 |

You should answer **either**

Section 1:     Buddhism

**or**

Section 2:     Christianity

**or**

Section 3:     Hinduism

**or**

Section 4:     Islam

**or**

Section 5:     Judaism

**or**

Section 6:     Sikhism

The skills of knowledge and understanding (KU) and analysis and evaluation (AE) are being assessed in this paper. When answering each question you should note the number of marks allocated to each skill as indicated after each part of the question.

## Section 1 – Buddhism

*Marks Code*

**Reminder:** *You should choose this section if you have studied* **Buddhism** *in the World Religion Unit.*

**Instructions:** Answer **all** the questions. The marks available for each question are indicated. Use these as a guide to the amount of detail you should include in your answer.

1. (*a*) Describe the law of Kamma.

   **6 KU**

   (*b*) Explain the benefits that belief in Kamma might bring Buddhists.

   **4 AE**

   (*c*) Explain the difficulties that belief in Kamma might create for Buddhists.

   **4 AE**

2. (*a*) By what means do Buddhists believe they can achieve the goals of life?

   **8 KU**

   (*b*) How important is the Dhamma in the lives of Buddhists?

   **4 AE**

3. (*a*) What do Buddhists believe about anatta?

   **6 KU**

   (*b*) "For Buddhists, anatta is the key to understanding the human condition."
   How far do you agree?

   **8 AE**

   **(40)**

**Section 2 – Christianity**                                    *Marks Code*

**Reminder:** *You should choose this section if you have studied **Christianity** in the World Religion Unit.*

**Instructions:** Answer **all** the questions. The marks available for each question are indicated. Use these as a guide to the amount of detail you should include in your answer.

1. (*a*) What example did Jesus set for Christians in his life and teachings?                                    **6 KU**

   (*b*) Explain the benefits that following Jesus' teachings might bring Christians.                                    **4 AE**

   (*c*) Explain the difficulties that following Jesus' teachings might create for Christians.                                    **4 AE**

2. (*a*) By what means do Christians believe they can achieve the goals of life?                                    **8 KU**

   (*b*) How important is belief in salvation in the lives of Christians?                                    **4 AE**

3. (*a*) What do Christians believe about freewill?                                    **6 KU**

   (*b*) "For Christians, freewill is the key to understanding the human condition."

   How far do you agree?                                    **8 AE**

                                    **(40)**

**[Turn over**

## Section 3 – Hinduism

*Marks  Code*

**Reminder:**  *You should choose this section if you have studied **Hinduism** in the World Religion Unit.*

**Instructions:**  Answer **all** the questions.  The marks available for each question are indicated.  Use these as a guide to the amount of detail you should include in your answer.

1.  (*a*)  Describe what Hindus understand by dharma.

    **6  KU**

    (*b*)  Explain the benefits that dharma might bring Hindus.

    **4  AE**

    (*c*)  Explain the difficulties that dharma might create for Hindus.

    **4  AE**

2.  (*a*)  By what means do Hindus believe they can achieve the goals of life?

    **8  KU**

    (*b*)  How important is detachment in the lives of Hindus?

    **4  AE**

3.  (*a*)  What do Hindus believe about the atman?

    **6  KU**

    (*b*)  "For Hindus, knowing the nature of the atman is the key to understanding the human condition."

    How far do you agree?

    **8  AE**

    **(40)**

## Section 4 – Islam

*Marks  Code*

**Reminder:**  *You should choose this section if you have studied **Islam** in the World Religion Unit.*

**Instructions:**  Answer **all** the questions.  The marks available for each question are indicated.  Use these as a guide to the amount of detail you should include in your answer.

1. (*a*)  Describe Muslim beliefs about Akhirah.                              **6  KU**

   (*b*)  Explain the benefits that belief in Akhirah might bring Muslims.    **4  AE**

   (*c*)  Explain the difficulties that belief in Akhirah might create for Muslims.  **4  AE**

2. (*a*)  By what means do Muslims believe they can achieve the goals of life?  **8  KU**

   (*b*)  How important is the Qur'an in the lives of Muslims?                **4  AE**

3. (*a*)  What do Muslims believe about suffering and disobedience?          **6  KU**

   (*b*)  "For Muslims, disobedience is the key to understanding the human condition."

      How far do you agree?                                                  **8  AE**

                                                                          **(40)**

**[Turn over**

## Section 5 – Judaism

Marks   Code

**Reminder:** *You should choose this section if you have studied **Judaism** in the World Religion Unit.*

**Instructions:** Answer **all** the questions. The marks available for each question are indicated. Use these as a guide to the amount of detail you should include in your answer.

1. (a) Describe Jewish beliefs about the Covenant.                                                          6   KU

   (b) Explain the benefits that living according to the Covenant might bring Jews.                                                                              4   AE

   (c) Explain the difficulties that living according to the Covenant might create for Jews.                                                                        4   AE

2. (a) By what means do Jews believe they can achieve the goals of life?                                     8   KU

   (b) How important is Lashon Harah in the lives of Jews?                              4   AE

3. (a) What do Jews believe about humanity's dual nature?                                 6   KU

   (b) "For Jews, humanity's dual nature is the key to understanding the human condition."

      How far do you agree?                                                                                    8   AE

                                                                                                         **(40)**

**Section 6 – Sikhism**                                              *Marks   Code*

**Reminder:** *You should choose this section if you have studied* **Sikhism** *in the World Religion Unit.*

**Instructions:** Answer **all** the questions. The marks available for each question are indicated. Use these as a guide to the amount of detail you should include in your answer.

1. (*a*)  Describe Sikh beliefs about Gurmukh.                                6   **KU**

   (*b*)  Explain the benefits that becoming Gurmukh might bring Sikhs.       4   **AE**

   (*c*)  Explain the difficulties that becoming Gurmukh might create for Sikhs.   4   **AE**

2. (*a*)  By what means do Sikhs believe they can achieve the goals of life?   8   **KU**

   (*b*)  How important is the Living Guru in the lives of Sikhs?            4   **AE**

3. (*a*)  What do Sikhs believe about karma?                                  6   **KU**

   (*b*)  "For Sikhs, karma is the key to understanding the human condition."
          How far do you agree?                                              8   **AE**

                                                                            **(40)**

*[END OF QUESTION PAPER]*

[BLANK PAGE]

**[BLANK PAGE]**

# X265/12/01

| NATIONAL QUALIFICATIONS 2013 | MONDAY, 3 JUNE 1.00 PM – 2.45 PM | RELIGIOUS, MORAL AND PHILOSOPHICAL STUDIES HIGHER Paper 1 |
|---|---|---|

**There are two Sections in this paper:**

Section 1 – Morality in the Modern World
Section 2 – Christianity:  Belief and Science

Section 1:  You should only answer all the questions on the topic you have studied.

Topic 1 – Crime and Punishment **or**
Topic 2 – Gender **or**
Topic 3 – Global Issues **or**
Topic 4 – Medical Ethics **or**
Topic 5 – War and Peace.

Section 2:  All questions are mandatory.

The skills of knowledge and understanding (KU) and analysis and evaluation (AE) are being assessed in this paper.  When answering each question you should note the number of marks allocated to each skill as indicated after each part of the question.

## SECTION 1

*Marks*    *Code*

### Morality in the Modern World

#### Topic 1 – Crime and Punishment

**Reminder:** *Topic 1 is for candidates who have studied* **Crime and Punishment** *in the Morality in the Modern World Unit.*

**Instructions:** Answer **all** the questions. The marks available for each question are indicated. You should use these as a guide to the amount of detail you should include in your answer.

1.   (*a*)   What is meant by "respect of persons" in Kantian Ethics?      **3**    **KU**

     (*b*)   Describe Utilitarian ethics.      **4**    **KU**

     (*c*)   What is meant by reformation?      **3**    **KU**

     (*d*)   Explain Utilitarian views on the purposes of punishment.      **4**    **AE**

2.   (*a*)   What is meant by economic causes of crime?      **4**    **KU**

     (*b*)   "Economic factors are no excuse for committing crimes."

        Explain how this view can be justified.      **6**    **AE**

3.   (*a*)   Describe **two** religious responses to the issue of abolishing the death penalty.      **6**    **KU**

     (*b*)   To what extent do you agree with these religious responses?      **10**    **AE**

                                                 **(40)**

**Topic 2 – Gender**                                            *Marks   Code*

**Reminder:** *Topic 2 is for candidates who have studied **Gender** in the Morality in the Modern World Unit.*

**Instructions:** Answer **all** the questions. The marks available for each question are indicated. You should use these as a guide to the amount of detail you should include in your answer.

1. (*a*) What is meant by "respect of persons" in Kantian Ethics?                    3   **KU**

   (*b*) Describe Utilitarian ethics.                                                 4   **KU**

   (*c*) What is the role of the Equality and Human Rights Commission (EHRC) in relation to gender issues?                                          3   **KU**

   (*d*) Explain Utilitarian views on gender issues in the UK.                        4   **AE**

2. (*a*) What is meant by the empowerment of women?                                   4   **KU**

   (*b*) "In the UK the empowerment of men is just as important as the empowerment of women."

   Explain how this view can be justified.                                           6   **AE**

3. (*a*) Describe **two** religious responses to the issue of violence against women in the developing world.                                          6   **KU**

   (*b*) To what extent do you agree with these religious responses?                 10   **AE**

                                                                                    (40)

                                                          **[Turn over**

## Topic 3 – Global Issues

*Marks*   *Code*

**Reminder:** *Topic 3 is for candidates who have studied* **Global Issues** *in the Morality in the Modern World Unit.*

**Instructions:** Answer **all** the questions. The marks available for each question are indicated. You should use these as a guide to the amount of detail you should include in your answer.

1. (a) What is meant by "respect of persons" in Kantian Ethics?    **3   KU**

   (b) Describe Utilitarian ethics.    **4   KU**

   (c) What are the causes of poverty?    **3   KU**

   (d) Explain Utilitarian views on the global distribution of wealth and resources.    **4   AE**

2. (a) What is meant by "aid"?    **4   KU**

   (b) "Conditions should be attached to all aid given to poor countries."

   Explain how this view can be justified.    **6   AE**

3. (a) Describe **two** religious responses to the issue of stewardship of the environment.    **6   KU**

   (b) To what extent do you agree with these religious responses?    **10   AE**

   **(40)**

## Topic 4 – Medical Ethics

*Marks   Code*

**Reminder:**   *Topic 4 is for candidates who have studied* **Medical Ethics** *in the Morality in the Modern World Unit.*

**Instructions:**   Answer **all** the questions.  The marks available for each question are indicated.  You should use these as a guide to the amount of detail you should include in your answer.

1.  (*a*)  What is meant by "respect of persons" in Kantian Ethics?                    3   **KU**

    (*b*)  Describe Utilitarian ethics.                    4   **KU**

    (*c*)  In what situations has voluntary euthanasia been used?                    3   **KU**

    (*d*)  Explain Utilitarian views on euthanasia.                    4   **AE**


2.  (*a*)  What is involved in embryonic stem cell research?                    4   **KU**

    (*b*)  "Embryonic stem cell research is a necessary evil."

       Explain how this view can be justified.                    6   **AE**


3.  (*a*)  Describe **two** religious responses to the issue of non-voluntary euthanasia.                    6   **KU**

    (*b*)  To what extent do you agree with these religious responses?                    10   **AE**

                    **(40)**


                    **[Turn over**

## Topic 5 – War and Peace　　　　　　　　　　*Marks　Code*

**Reminder:** *Topic 5 is for candidates who have studied* **War and Peace** *in the Morality in the Modern World Unit.*

**Instructions:** Answer **all** the questions. The marks available for each question are indicated. You should use these as a guide to the amount of detail you should include in your answer.

1. (*a*) What is meant by "respect of persons" in Kantian Ethics?　　3　**KU**

　　(*b*) Describe Utilitarian ethics.　　4　**KU**

　　(*c*) In what ways do countries respond to aggression?　　3　**KU**

　　(*d*) Explain Utilitarian responses to war.　　4　**AE**

2. (*a*) What is meant by chemical weapons?　　4　**KU**

　　(*b*) "Chemical weapons should have a place in modern warfare."
　　　　Explain how this view can be justified.　　6　**AE**

3. (*a*) Describe **two** religious responses to the issue of using conventional weapons.　　6　**KU**

　　(*b*) To what extent do you agree with these religious responses?　　10　**AE**

　　　　　　　　　　　　　　　　　　　　　　　　　　**(40)**

*[END OF SECTION 1]*

## SECTION 2

*Marks   Code*

### Christianity: Belief and Science

**Reminder:** *This section should be answered by all candidates.*

**Instructions:** Answer **all** the questions. The marks available for each question are indicated. You should use these as a guide to the amount of detail you should include in your answer.

1. (*a*) What methods do scientists use to make sense of reality?                  4   KU

   (*b*) Explain **two** limitations of these methods.                  4   AE

2. (*a*) Describe how science explains the origin of the universe.                  4   KU

   (*b*) Give **two** reasons why some Christians accept the scientific view of the origin of the universe.                  4   KU

   (*c*) Explain why some Christians might challenge these two reasons.                  6   AE

3. (*a*) What evidence do literalist Christians use to support belief that God created humans?                  4   KU

   (*b*) What evidence do scientists use to support evolutionary theory?                  4   KU

   (*c*) "Evolution alone is not enough to explain the origin of human life."

   How far do you agree?                  10   AE

   **(40)**

*[END OF SECTION 2]*

*[END OF QUESTION PAPER]*

[BLANK PAGE]

# X265/12/02

| NATIONAL QUALIFICATIONS 2013 | MONDAY, 3 JUNE 3.05 PM – 4.00 PM | RELIGIOUS, MORAL AND PHILOSOPHICAL STUDIES HIGHER Paper 2 |

You should answer **either**

Section 1:     Buddhism

**or**

Section 2:     Christianity

**or**

Section 3:     Hinduism

**or**

Section 4:     Islam

**or**

Section 5:     Judaism

**or**

Section 6:     Sikhism

The skills of knowledge and understanding (KU) and analysis and evaluation (AE) are being assessed in this paper.  When answering each question you should note the number of marks allocated to each skill as indicated after each part of the question.

## Section 1 – Buddhism

Marks   Code

**Reminder:** *You should choose this section if you have studied* **Buddhism** *in the World Religion Unit.*

**Instructions:** Answer **all** the questions. The marks available for each question are indicated. Use these as a guide to the amount of detail you should include in your answer.

1.  (*a*)  What do Buddhists understand by skilful actions?          4   **KU**

    (*b*)  Describe Buddhist meditation.          4   **KU**

    (*c*)  How important is Buddhist meditation as a means of developing skilful actions?          4   **AE**

2.  (*a*)  Describe Buddhist beliefs about the Three Root Poisons.          3   **KU**

    (*b*)  What do Buddhists believe about Samsara?          3   **KU**

    (*c*)  Explain the challenges belief in the Three Root Poisons and Samsara present to Buddhists.          6   **AE**

3.  (*a*)  Describe the dhamma.          6   **KU**

    (*b*)  Why might Buddhists believe that the dhamma is still relevant today?          10   **AE**

          **(40)**

## Section 2 – Christianity

*Marks  Code*

**Reminder:**  *You should choose this section if you have studied* **Christianity** *in the World Religion Unit.*

**Instructions:**  Answer **all** the questions.  The marks available for each question are indicated.  Use these as a guide to the amount of detail you should include in your answer.

1.  (*a*)  What do Christians mean by developing a relationship with God?  **4   KU**

    (*b*)  What do Christians understand by the Christian Community?  **4   KU**

    (*c*)  How important is the Christian Community in developing a relationship with God?  **4   AE**

2.  (*a*)  Describe what Christians believe about sin.  **3   KU**

    (*b*)  What do Christians believe about the nature of God?  **3   KU**

    (*c*)  Explain the challenges beliefs about sin and the nature of God present to Christians.  **6   AE**

3.  (*a*)  Describe the suffering and death of Jesus.  **6   KU**

    (*b*)  Why might Christians believe that the suffering and death of Jesus is still relevant today?  **10   AE**

    **(40)**

**[Turn over**

**Section 3 – Hinduism**                                    *Marks   Code*

**Reminder:**  *You should choose this section if you have studied* **Hinduism** *in the World Religion Unit.*

**Instructions:**  Answer **all** the questions.  The marks available for each question are indicated.  Use these as a guide to the amount of detail you should include in your answer.

1.  (*a*)  Describe Hindu beliefs about moksha.                          **4    KU**

    (*b*)  What do Hindus understand by the term detachment?            **4    KU**

    (*c*)  How important is detachment for achieving moksha?            **4    AE**

2.  (*a*)  Describe what Hindus understand by maya.                      **3    KU**

    (*b*)  What do Hindus believe about avidya?                          **3    KU**

    (*c*)  Explain the challenges beliefs about maya and avidya present to Hindus.  **6    AE**

3.  (*a*)  In what ways do Hindus practise bhakti marga?                 **6    KU**

    (*b*)  Why might Hindus believe that bhakti marga is still relevant today?  **10   AE**

                                                                        **(40)**

## Section 4 – Islam

*Marks Code*

**Reminder:** *You should choose this section if you have studied **Islam** in the World Religion Unit.*

**Instructions:** Answer **all** the questions. The marks available for each question are indicated. Use these as a guide to the amount of detail you should include in your answer.

1. (*a*) In what ways do Muslims describe Paradise?      4 KU

     (*b*) What is the Sunnah?      4 KU

     (*c*) How important is following the Sunnah for Muslims to secure the reward of Paradise?      4 AE

2. (*a*) Describe what Muslims believe about the nature of human beings.      3 KU

     (*b*) What do Muslims believe about predestination?      3 KU

     (*c*) Explain the challenges beliefs about the nature of human being and predestination present to Muslims.      6 AE

3. (*a*) What is involved in observing Salah?      6 KU

     (*b*) Why might Muslims believe that Salah is still relevant today?      10 AE

                                                      **(40)**

**[Turn over**

## Section 5 – Judaism

Marks   Code

**Reminder:** *You should choose this section if you have studied **Judaism** in the World Religion Unit.*

**Instructions:** Answer **all** the questions. The marks available for each question are indicated. Use these as a guide to the amount of detail you should include in your answer.

1.  (a) What do Jews understand by the Messianic Age?

    **4   KU**

    (b) What do Jews understand by the Ten Commandments?

    **4   KU**

    (c) How important are the Ten Commandments in bringing about the Messianic Age?

    **4   AE**

2.  (a) Describe Jewish beliefs about suffering.

    **3   KU**

    (b) What do Jews believe about the nature of God?

    **3   KU**

    (c) Explain the challenges beliefs about suffering and the nature of God present to Jews.

    **6   AE**

3.  (a) In what ways do Jews observe Shabbat?

    **6   KU**

    (b) Why might Jews believe that Shabbat is still relevant today?

    **10   AE**

    **(40)**

## Section 6 – Sikhism

*Marks   Code*

**Reminder:** *You should choose this section if you have studied* **Sikhism** *in the World Religion Unit.*

**Instructions:** Answer **all** the questions. The marks available for each question are indicated. Use these as a guide to the amount of detail you should include in your answer.

1. (*a*)  What do Sikhs understand by jivan mukhti?                                                    4    KU

   (*b*)  Describe Sikh beliefs about equality.                                                           4    KU

   (*c*)  How important are beliefs about equality in bringing Sikhs closer to jivan mukhti?                                                                                  4    AE

2. (*a*)  Describe what Sikhs believe about maya.                                                      3    KU

   (*b*)  What do Sikhs believe about haumai?                                                            3    KU

   (*c*)  Explain the challenges beliefs about maya and haumai present to Sikhs.            6    AE

3. (*a*)  What obligations do Sikhs have as members of the Khalsa?                             6    KU

   (*b*)  Why might Sikhs believe that the Khalsa is still relevant today?                   10    AE

                                                                                                                       (40)

*[END OF QUESTION PAPER]*

[BLANK PAGE]

# SQA HIGHER RELIGIOUS, MORAL & PHILOSOPHICAL STUDIES, SPECIMEN QUESTION PAPER 2010–2013

## RM&PS HIGHER
## PAPER 1
## SPECIMEN MARKING INSTRUCTIONS 2010

**Weighting of questions:**

*Knowledge and Understanding – approximately 50% of total marks available. The generic requirement for KU is that accurate, relevant and detailed knowledge of content is demonstrated; the information is presented in a coherent manner and information is communicated effectively using accurate terminology.*

*Analysis and Evaluation – approximately 50% of total marks available. The generic requirement for AE is for analysis of concepts, processes, evidence etc to be shown and evaluation to be balanced and informed.*

*Where candidates refer to appropriate sacred writings credit will be given. As a general guide a relevant and appropriate reference (which can be paraphrased or verbatim) will gain one mark. Where it is clearly applied to a concept or point it will receive a further mark. There is no limit on the number of references that can be used in an answer. However, relevance and appropriateness is essential.*
*No marks will be awarded where candidates simply provide a list. Any terms listed must be accompanied by a brief explanation to gain a mark. The bullet points under the questions are a guide as to the areas that candidates may discuss in their answers. The examples are neither mandatory nor exhaustive.*
*Where candidates introduce new KU into an AE answer to make or support a point credit should be given.*
*Candidates will not be awarded marks for KU which has been used elsewhere within a question.*

# SECTION 1

## TOPIC 1: CRIME AND PUNISHMENT

1. (a) • Plato told the story
   • Socrates and Euthyphro at court
   • Who decides what is right?
   • Do moral rules come from God?
   • Do moral rules come from elsewhere and God recognises them as good? **KU3**

   (b) • Depends on the religion
   • Depends on status of sacred writing in religions
   • Source of moral teaching
   • Morality developed from sacred writings
   • Sacred writings used to help form basis of response to new issues
   • Literal understanding leads to literal obedience to morality **KU4**

   (c) • Consequentialist
   • Greatest benefit for greatest number
   • Act
   • Rule
   • Bentham and/or Mill developed it **KU3**

   (d) *Candidates should not receive marks for KU used in question 1(c). Where new KU is introduced and used to make an AE point a mark should be awarded.*
   • If it deters future criminals it is good
   • If it allows justice to be seen to be done and reassures us all it is good
   • If it produces unhappiness because an innocent person has been executed it is bad

• If it is used indiscriminately and poses a threat to us all it is bad **AE4**

2. (a) *Maximum of two marks for each court sentence. Where more than two sentences are described the best two descriptions should be awarded marks.*
   • Fines: fines levied on the offender to be paid over a period of time determined by the court
   • Community Service: supervised work in the community
   • Imprisonment: detention for a time determined by the court
   • Restraining Orders: includes injunctions not to go to certain place, sex offenders' register and tagging **KU4**

   (b) • Failed reformation
   • Failed deterrence. High percentage of criminals re-offend within 2 years thus ineffective
   • Failed retribution. Criminal does not get the 'eye for an eye' treatment

3. (a) *There can be a considerable number of initiatives discussed in this answer and they may fall under the following broad headings. Candidates may gain marks for describing one in detail or several more briefly.*
   • Government responses – e.g. increased policing, family support, community initiatives, alternatives to custody, children's justice system
   • NGO responses – e.g. charitable youth work, lobbying, family support, offender and victim support
   • Religious responses – e.g. youth work, inner city work, family support, offender and victim support **KU6**

   (b) *Whilst a number of causes are specified in the arrangements, candidates may identify causes other than those in the arrangements in this answer. It is expected that candidates will write two or three reasons for this answer. It is also possible for candidates to discuss one concern in depth and gain full marks.*
   • Breakdown of the family
   • Loss of mutual love and respect in society
   • They affect the disadvantaged more than anyone
   • Causes could be breaking religious morality
   • Golden Rule is challenged
   • Religion may have caused the crime
   • Issues relating to justice **AE8**

## TOPIC 2: GENDER ISSUES

1. (a) • Plato told the story
   • Socrates and Euthyphro at court
   • Who decides what is right?
   • Do moral rules come from God?
   • Do moral rules come from elsewhere and God recognises them as good? **KU3**

   (b) • Depends on the religion
   • Depends on status of sacred writing in religions
   • Source of moral teaching
   • Morality developed from sacred writings
   • Sacred writings used to help form basis of response to new issues
   • Literal understanding leads to literal obedience to morality **KU4**

   (c) • Consequentialist
   • Greatest benefit for greatest number
   • Act
   • Rule
   • Bentham and/or Mill developed it **KU3**

(d) • Equality will promote greater happiness in society
    • Equality releases potential which will benefit society
    • Equality brings fairness which makes more people content with their position in society
    • Stereotyping treats people as an anonymous group not as individuals
    • Stereotyping does not maximise happiness for most because it is based on generalisations which do not take account of individuality
    • Reject any distinctions as to who is equal and who is not – **all** are equal
    • They reject all forms of discrimination found in gender or elsewhere     **AE4**

2. (a) • Supportive role to male leader
    • Helpless and lacking guile
    • Emotional
    • Dependent
    • Promiscuous
    • Body portrayals     **KU4**

  (b) • Inaccurate portrayal of women as they really are in society
    • Inaccurate message to society leading to certain expectations of women
    • Low self-esteem leading to reduced ambitions
    • Sexual vulnerability due to sexual promiscuity portrayed in the media
    • Social constraints leading to reduced opportunities in life     **AE8**

3. (a) *There can be a considerable number of examples discussed in this answer. Candidates may gain marks for describing one in detail or several more briefly.*
    • Domestic violence e.g. the cultural traditions that permit it in Asia and Africa
    • Sexual violence e.g. genital mutilation in parts of Africa
    • Female infanticide in parts of Asia and Africa
    • Military violence against women e.g. Rwanda
    • Penal violence against women e.g. Somalia     **KU6**

  (b) *It is expected that candidates will write two or three reasons for this answer. It is also possible for candidates to discuss one concern in depth and gain full marks.*
    • Equal in the eyes of God
    • Unjust – God is a God of justice in all religions
    • Murder is wrong
    • Golden Rule is broken
    • Religion may promote it
    • Religion may condone it
    • Religion my turn a blind eye to it     **AE8**

## TOPIC 3: GLOBAL ISSUES

1. (a) • Plato told the story
    • Socrates and Euthyphro at court
    • Who decides what is right?
    • Do moral rules come from God?
    • Do moral rules come from elsewhere and God recognises them as good?     **KU3**

  (b) • Depends on the religion
    • Depends on status of sacred writing in religions
    • Source of moral teaching
    • Morality developed from sacred writings
    • Sacred writings used to help form basis of response to new issues
    • Literal understanding leads to literal obedience to morality     **KU4**

  (c) • Consequentialist
    • Greatest benefit for greatest number
    • Act
    • Rule
    • Bentham and/or Mill developed it     **KU3**

(d) • Globalisation is good if it increases the happiness of all those who give and receive it
    • The interest of the community is the sum interest of its members thus as members of the world community we should be interested in maximising profit and reducing costs
    • Against it because fewer benefit from it then suffer as a result
    • Against it because it promotes suffering of the majority     **AE4**

2. (a) • Burning fossil fuels in generating power, transport and manufacturing
    • Methane production farming, burning fossil fuels and bacteria
    • Nitrous oxide production through fertilisers, burning organic matter, cars, nylon and acid production
    • Deforestation – burning releases carbon dioxide and ability of the planet to absorb it     **KU4**

  (b) • Climate change affecting cycles of seasons, introducing extreme weather
    • Glacial retreat affecting sea levels and temperatures
    • Ocean – acidified leading to reduction in biodiversity
    • Impact on the global economy as infrastructure and industry is affected     **AE8**

3. (a) *There can be a considerable number of examples discussed in this answer. Candidates may gain marks for describing one in detail or several more briefly.*
    • Transforming a local or regional business into a worldwide concern
    • World Bank was created to play a role in globalisation
    • WTO is part of globalisation
    • IMF is part of the global banking system
    • Provision of goods and services on a global scale e.g. hotels
    • Migrating work forces
    • Distribution of capital
    • Sharing of research and resources     **KU6**

  (b) *It is expected that candidates will write two or three reasons for this answer. It is also possible for candidates to discuss one concern in depth and gain full marks.*
    • Different religions are the basis of different societies, globalisation challenges that
    • Globalisation has led to secularisation and the loss of spiritual values and experience
    • Can lead to fundamentalism as cultures try to re-assert their traditional values
    • Devalues the individual in favour of the corporate dream
    • Examples of unscrupulous suppliers to global names abound
    • Globalisation benefits the developed world, not the developing world – does not promote equality
    • Internal conflict in religion between modernists and traditionalists e.g. Afghanistan     **AE8**

## TOPIC 4: MEDICAL ETHICS

1. (a) • Plato told the story
    • Socrates and Euthyphro at court
    • Who decides what is right?
    • Do moral rules come from God?
    • Do moral rules come from elsewhere and God recognises them as good?     **KU3**

  (b) • Depends on the religion
    • Depends on status of sacred writing in religions
    • Source of moral teaching
    • Morality developed from sacred writings
    • Sacred writings used to help form basis of response to new issues
    • Literal understanding leads to literal obedience to morality     **KU4**

(c) • Consequentialist
• Greatest benefit for greatest number
• Act
• Rule
• Bentham and/or Mill developed it     **KU3**

(d) • Happiness is maximised and pain is minimised in the case of a terminally ill patient
• The death of the patient brings benefits to the many others needing treatment and a hospital bed
• Some might say that fear of being euthanized means a utilitarian can't support it – can support it because it is an individual not an arbitrary decision
• Euthanasia is right because at a stroke it reduces the suffering in the world
• Mill said humans are autonomous – what we do with our own body is our decision nobody else's
• Bentham said the law should deal with people's actions and not moral decisions – individual's choice, law has no business being there
• Act – says it is right if the benefits outweigh the benefits of the alternative action
• Rule – generalised set of rules may mean that they can support voluntary euthanasia because it upholds individual autonomy but it cannot support involuntary euthanasia because of its removal of autonomous decisions     **AE4**

2. (a) • Prevention of inherited disease being passed on
• Infertility – to help couples have children
• Impotence – to help couples have children
• Gender selection – to select a particular gender for medical or other reasons of choice
• Experimentation – to use embryos for scientific research     **KU4**

(b) • Variable success rate
• High wastage of embryos
• Cost effectiveness
• Open to abuse
• Problems related to definitions of the beginning of life
• Considered to be un-natural by some     **AE8**

3. (a) *There can be a considerable number of examples discussed in this answer. Candidates may gain marks for describing one in detail or several more briefly.*
• Individual asks for euthanasia
• Individual requests euthanasia through an advanced directive or living will
Worked examples may include:
• Terminally ill patient who asks to be allowed to die
• Terminally ill patient who asks to be killed
• Healthy person who leaves an advanced directive     **KU6**

(b) *It is expected that candidates will write two or three reasons for this answer. It is also possible for candidates to discuss one concern in depth and gain full marks.*
• It is murder
• Interferes with the will of God
• Interferes with God's purpose for our lives
• Suffering has a value, this denies its value
• Concern over the vulnerable
• Concern over the patient-doctor relationship     **AE8**

**TOPIC 5: WAR AND PEACE**

1. (a) • Plato told the story
• Socrates and Euthyphro at court
• Who decides what is right?
• Do moral rules come from God?
• Do moral rules come from elsewhere and God recognises them as good?     **KU3**

(b) • Depends on the religion
• Depends on status of sacred writing in religions
• Source of moral teaching
• Morality developed from sacred writings
• Sacred writings used to help form basis of response to new issues
• Literal understanding leads to literal obedience to morality     **KU4**

(c) • Consequentialist
• Greatest benefit for greatest number
• Act
• Rule
• Bentham and/or Mill developed it     **KU3**

(d) **Support wars**
• They might support a war despite the issues arising from it because the greatest good would be to have peace in the long-term
• Even though a minority may be against the war they could still have their views respected, they could be conscientious objectors
• It would be for the greatest good for the greatest number in a society to get rid of a dictator who was abusing the human rights of civilians
• Utilitarians would recognise that it would make most people happy to have peace but people also want to have justice
• Utilitarians might support possessing WMD as a deterrent. It would be for the greater good of your country if it secured peace
• Utilitarians might not want to be pacifist on all occasions as this could lead you to be vulnerable to attack by countries that see you as a soft touch

**Oppose wars**
• Utilitarians might oppose war because of the issues that arise from it. Violence leads to more violence. This is not in the interests of the majority
• Modern weapons like WMD mean the effects of war are even more devastating
• The money used to fund war would be better spent on providing the basics for everyone e.g. shelter, healthcare, food and clean water
• Utilitarians might not want to be drawn into conflicts where you are supporting allies. They might think it is more realistic to look after the happiness of people in your own country than on a global scale     **AE4**

2. (a) • You have been invaded or threatened by another power and respond in self-defence
• Struggle for peace
• Fighting for scarce resources (land, oil etc)
• Fighting to support your allies
• Fighting for religious or political beliefs
• Fighting to prevent a country developing nuclear weapons
• Fighting to protect innocent people and uphold human rights     **KU4**

(b) • Financial cost. War is expensive
• This money could have been spent on the root cause of the conflict instead and avoided the bloodshed
• Taxes being diverted from social institutions like schools and hospitals
• Human cost. War always results in loss of life
• It is not just loss of servicemen. Many innocent civilians are also killed
• Environmental cost. War damages the environment, especially with WMD like nuclear weapons
• Infrastructure is destroyed and needs to be rebuilt     **AE8**

3. (a) *There can be a considerable number of examples discussed in this answer. Candidates may gain marks for describing one in detail or several more briefly.*
   - Biological weapons like anthrax
   - Chemical weapons like mustard gas
   - Nuclear weapons like the nuclear bombs dropped on Nagasaki and Hiroshima        **KU6**

   (b) *It is expected that candidates will write two or three reasons for this answer. It is also possible for candidates to discuss one concern in depth and gain full marks.*
   - WMD are very expensive. This money could have been spent on solving the root cause of conflicts instead
   - WMD are indiscriminate. Huge loss of innocent lives
   - WMD wipes out all life in the surrounding area. This could be seen as taking God's power
   - Loss of life through their use is significant because life is sacred/special
   - Goes against religious teachings e.g. Love thy neighbour
   - Goes against the example of pacifist religious leaders
   - WMD have long-lasting effects on the environment which doesn't fulfil our responsibility to look after the world
   - Even if WMD don't kill they cause great suffering for people at the time and in the future e.g. high cancer rates in Japan long after the bombings of Hiroshima and Nagasaki        **AE8**

## SECTION 2

1. (a) *Candidates may obtain a maximum of 2 marks for each description.*

   **General ...Revelatio Realis**
   - Revelation through Nature (the works of God)
   - To people in general
   - Is rooted in creation and addressed to human reason, conscience, right/wrong and experience

   **Special ...Revelatio Verbalis**
   - Revelation through Scripture (the word of God)
   - A particular communication to a particular individual e.g. a dream, vision, miracle ... Moses – burning bush, Saul on the road to Damascus etc
   - Is seen as an extension of religious experience
   - Is rooted in God's plan to redeem us ... is addressed to man as a sinner and can be understood by faith        **KU4**

   (b) • A four stage process of ... Observation, Hypothesis, Experiment, Verification
   - Study the natural world in a systematic way
   - Based on evidence and experiment
   - Induction, deduction and verification
   - Provides data which can be independently tested by other scientists
   - Tentative        **KU4**

   (c) *Candidates should discuss two differences only with a maximum of three marks for each.*
   - Science looks to understand the 'HOW' questions of the nature of reality – religion looks at why
   - Science can provide data which can be independently tested by other scientists – religious claims cannot be empirically tested
   - Science is a good basis on which to build our knowledge of the world and how it operates – religion depends on more speculative answers
   - Science has the capacity to change as new ideas, information become available – religion is not as open to new ideas and change
   - Religion answers questions about meaning, value and purpose – science does not

   - Religion can demonstrate the existence of God – science has no means of testing this hypothesis
   - Religion takes reality as a whole, science is reductionist in its approach
   - Religion is subjective; science objective        **AE6**

2. (a) *Candidates may give four or more pieces of supporting evidence and should receive full marks for a detailed description.*
   - Redshift of galaxies
   - Background radiation
   - Proportion of primordial elements
   - Shape and form of galaxies
   - Cosmic evolution        **KU4**

   (b) *Candidates may answer by describing the Genesis 1 creation story.*
   - Took six days to create
   - It was void and formless
   - God imposed order
   - Description of each day's activities
   - Created on God's command
   - Created with ease        **KU4**

   (c) **Creationist Response**
   - Scripture is fact ... Big Bang is a theory ... It may be falsified at a later date
   - Science has been wrong in the past
   - The Bible contains no errors ... It is the revealed Word of God
   - Belief in what the Bible says is more important than scientific discoveries/evidence
   - Young earth suggested by the Bible

   **Conservative Response**
   - Big Bang could be God's method, cannot rule it out
   - Big Bang establishes that universe had a beginning so it is a possibility
   - Fact of creation is more important than method of creation
   - Young earth does not match the evidence of science
   - God created world in six day-ages or stages, Big Bang is one of them

   **Liberal Response**
   - There is no contradiction ... The Big Bang is God's method
   - Revelation is contained in nature too ... 2 books ... Book of Scripture and the Book of nature
   - The Bible has to be seen in its context
   - Science can be revelation too        **AE6**

3. (a) • Stone on the heath
   - Conclusion about the stone
   - Design of watch
   - Conclusion about the watch
   - Complexity of human eye
   - Regularity of the seasons etc
   - Parallels with the above and world/universe
   - Complexities within nature
   - Comparison with God and the Universe
   - Therefore God exists        **KU4**

   (b) *Candidates should discuss two strengths and two weaknesses only. A maximum of four marks is available for explaining two strengths and four for two weaknesses. Within this figure a maximum of three marks can be given for any one strength or weakness.*

   **Strengths**
   - Uses objects which are familiar to us
   - Complexity exists ... There is an appearance of purpose in everything

- The human mind is predisposed to interpret events in an ordered way ... it infers the existence of God from the presence of order
- Order is seen as a mark of design ... design is also easy to see if you make your own existence the centre and purpose of the universe
- It is logical ... Some science can support it

**Weaknesses**

- Leap of faith
- Idea of the universe/life being a designed machine is not appropriate – it's more like a growing/developing organism in response to its environment
- Because certain parts of life appear to be designed doesn't mean the whole process is ... or in need of a designer
- There is a great deal of evidence of bad design... There is so much suffering and cruelty in nature
- A great deal of waste is involved in the process – opposite of organisation and design
- Apparent design can occur even if the process is subject to natural selection and adaptation. Life forms would not have survived without the ability to adapt **AE8**

# RM&PS HIGHER PAPER 2 SPECIMEN MARKING INSTRUCTIONS 2010

**Weighting of questions:**

*Knowledge and Understanding – approximately 50% of total marks available. The generic requirement for KU is that accurate, relevant and detailed knowledge of content is demonstrated; the information is presented in a coherent manner and information is communicated effectively using accurate terminology.*

*Analysis and Evaluation – approximately 50% of total marks available. The generic requirement for AE is for analysis of concepts, processes, evidence etc to be shown and evaluation to be balanced and informed.*

*Where candidates refer to appropriate sacred writings credit will be given. As a general guide a relevant and appropriate reference (which can be paraphrased or verbatim) will gain one mark. Where it is clearly applied to a concept or point it will receive a further mark. There is no limit on the number of references that can be used in an answer. However, relevance and appropriateness is essential.*

*No marks will be awarded where candidates simply provide a list. Any terms listed must be accompanied by a brief explanation to gain a mark. The bullet points under the questions are a guide as to the areas that candidates may discuss in their answers. The examples are neither mandatory nor exhaustive.*

*Where candidates introduce new KU into an AE answer to make or support a point credit should be given.*

*Candidates will not be awarded marks for KU which has been used elsewhere within a question.*

## SECTION 1: Buddhism

1. (a) • Greed – desire and attachment
   - Anger – rejection of things we do not like
   - Ignorance – not knowing our true nature
   - Stand in the way of a person's enlightenment
   - Keep wheel of samsara fuelled
   - Represented by cock, pig and snake **KU3**

   (b) *Maximum of two marks for each effect.*

   **Greed**
   - Attached to the material world
   - Desire (tanha) for things that we cannot have
   - Attached to impermanent things
   - Non acceptance of anicca and anatta
   - Bad kamma
   - Binds us to samsara
   - Cannot achieve Nibbana

   **Hatred**
   - Avoiding things we do not like
   - Wrong thoughts
   - Bad kamma
   - Binds us to samsara
   - Cannot achieve Nibbana

   **Ignorance**
   - Unaware of anatta and anicca
   - Delusion
   - Non acceptance of Buddhists' Way
   - Can't see our true nature
   - Restlessness and confusion
   - Binds us to samsara
   - Cannot achieve Nibbana **AE6**

2. (a) *It is important to note that candidates are not required to write six different points in this answer.*
   - It is rebirth
   - Part of the Second Noble Truth

- Karma affects samsara
- Power rather than soul moves on – anatta
- Theravadin view
- Mahayana view
- Cycle of birth, death and rebirth
- Ten realms of being     **KU6**

(b) *It is important to note that candidates are not required to write four different points in this answer.*
  - Can only be experienced
  - Not a place
  - Can be described through negative affirmation
  - Bliss
  - Cannot be described
  - Waking up to our true nature
  - Theravadin – arhats only
  - Mahayana – bodhisattva, open to all     **KU4**

(c) *It is important to note that candidates are not required to write six different points in this answer.*
  - Samsara is inclusive
  - Nibbana is exclusive because of its remoteness
  - Samsara gives individuals the goal of self improvement
  - Nibbana denies the existence of the self – hard to understand
  - Samsara demands that people act (kamma) – no special talent needed to take actions in life
  - Nibbana could be seen as making people withdraw – requires self discipline and sacrifice
  - Samsara involves community responsibility
  - Nibbana could be seen as a selfish pursuit
  - Samsara can stifle personal growth because it tells the individual to accept what they are
  - Nibbana brings peace and bliss     **AE6**

3. (a) • One who has achieved Enlightenment
  - Follows the Noble Eightfold Path
  - Follows the Five Precepts
  - Accepted the teachings of the Buddha
  - Lives as a monk
  - Meditates
  - Has no possessions
  - Theravadin ideal
  - Follows example of the Buddha     **KU3**

(b) • Historical development
  - Achieved enlightenment
  - Follows example of the Buddha
  - Delayed entry into Nibbana to help others
  - Compassionate Being
  - Mahayana ideal
  - Huge number of bodhisattvas celebrated in many Buddhists traditions     **KU4**

(c) *It is important to note that candidates are not required to write eight different points in this answer.*
  - Arhat is following the path of the Buddha
  - Arhat is the only person that can be fully committed to the Buddhist ideal
  - Arhat has devoted himself to the pursuit of Nibbana – lay people cannot do this
  - Arhat's life revolves around his religion
  - Bohhisattva is following the path of the Buddha because Buddha stayed and taught his followers
  - Bodhisattva is living on the Middle Way – arhats are extreme because asceticism is an extreme lifestyle
  - Bodhisattva's life is based on compassion – Buddha was compassionate
  - Buddha made his message for all – Bodhisattva does this too     **AE8**

# SECTION 2: Christianity

1. (a) • Special creation
  - Stewards of his creation
  - Loving relationship
  - Personal relationship
  - Alienated through sin
  - Redeemed through Jesus
  - Given us freewill so we can choose to accept and love God
  - God will not compel us to have a relationship with him     **KU3**

(b) *Maximum of two marks for each effect.*
  - There is hope for us
  - We can look forward to eternal life
  - We can love others as he loves us
  - We can overcome sin
  - We can overcome death
  - He has given humans his Word in the form of the Bible     **AE6**

2. (a) *It is important to note that candidates are not required to write six different points in this answer.*
  - Love God
  - Ask God's forgiveness
  - Love your neighbour
  - Treat others the way you want them to treat you
  - Sincerity is the key to one's relationship with God
  - Do not judge others
  - Love your enemies
  - Help the outcasts in society     **KU6**

(b) • No single idea of what it is
  - Biblical imagery of a place with celestial beings
  - State of being in God's presence forever
  - Characterised happiness and peace
  - Entry depends on faith and/or goodness
  - Entry gained only by the Elect/baptised/saved
  - Entry gained through God's grace     **KU4**

(c) *It is important to note that candidates are not required to write six different points in this answer.*
  - Depends on God's judgement of your life
  - Can lead a Christian lifestyle yet not believe so it is not enough
  - Must be part of the Christian community too
  - Relationship with God is essential to the Christian life so eternal life is only possible if this relationship exists
  - Acceptance of Jesus is essential to gaining salvation
  - Predestination – the kind of life you lead may make no difference
  - God's grace determines whether you get eternal life not just how you live your life
  - God's forgiveness is required for eternal life
  - Role of sacraments
  - Justification by faith     **AE6**

3. (a) • Outward sign that conveys an inward spiritual grace through Christ
  - Instituted by Christ
  - Carried out by clergy
  - Blessed elements, e.g. water, oil, bread, wine
  - Vows taken
  - RC Church has 7
  - Most have two, i.e. baptism and communion
  - Brief description of sacraments is acceptable     **KU3**

(b) • Lobbying
  - National and International Missions, e.g. Christian Aid, SCIAF
  - Support secular campaigns
  - Support charities
  - Personal commitment to local initiatives     **KU4**

(c) *It is important to note that candidates are not required to write eight different points in this answer.*
- Christian commitment is to follow the example of Jesus
- Jesus took action where he saw injustice
- Jesus criticised the piety of the Pharisees
- Christians are called to put their faith into action
- Christians should take part in both – room in their lives for both
- Christian teaching is meaningless unless it is put into action
- Social injustice is the concern of politicians not Christians
- Role is to 'tend the sick' rather than tackle the causes of the 'illness'
- Cannot live a full Christian life without the sacraments
- Could be said that sacraments demand Christian action
- Nothing is more important than being baptised in Jesus' name and breaking the bread in remembrance of him **AE8**

# SECTION 3: Hinduism

1. (a) *No marks for simply listing Gunas*
- Sattva – balance, order, purity
- Rajas – activity, restlessness
- Tamas – dullness, lethargy, slow **KU3**

(b) *Maximum of two marks for each effect*
**Sattva**
- Positive state of mind
- Orderly state of mind
- More able to see the true nature of the self
- Kind
- Calm
- Alert
- Thoughtful

**Rajas**
- Can be dynamic
- Can lead to desire
- Can lead to fear of losing what one desires
- Boldness

**Tamas**
- Inactive
- Unthinking
- Deluded
- Ignorant
- Self-destruction
- Negative

**General**
- Peace when the gunas are balanced
- When the balance is broken there are changes in matter or aspects of the world – they evolve in one way or another
- All three gunas are present in human beings who are bound to earthly existence if the gunas become unbalanced then a person becomes even more attached to the world **AE6**

2. (a) *It is important to note that candidates are not required to write six different points in this answer.*
- Permanent
- Changeless
- Brahman within
- Advaita – atman separate from jiva
- Visistadvaita – atman has essence from jiva
- Samkhya – atman is separate from prakrti
- Atman needs to be released
- Brahman and atman are one **KU6**

(b) • When the atman merges into Brahman
- It is an experience
- Can't be described

- Not a place
- Liberation from the cycle of samsara
- Freedom from pain and suffering
- Perfect bliss
- State of mind in this life/next life **KU4**

(c) *It is important to note that candidates are not required to write six different points in this answer.*
**Agree**
- Only a few people who are wholly spiritually devoted enter this spiritually devout stage
- Even for the most spiritual persons there is the risk that a person can become proud of their achievement and this would stop them from achieving moksha
- Only those that have dealt with the first three goals of Hinduism – dharma, artha and karma can begin the final stage of throwing off all earthly attachments and start the path of renunciation
- Very few people are able to do that because of family commitment and other duties and the pit falls of ignorance and doubt (avidya)
- Can't be achieved on earth because there will still be some avidya.
- Possible because great gurus have managed it.
- Some might say that moksha is beyond most people because we are easily distracted and get bound up with earthly existence which makes it very difficult to achieve the spiritual awareness that a Hindu needs to achieve moksha
- Whereas other Hindus believe that it is possible for some people to obtain liberation whilst still inhabiting a physical body
- It would certainly not be easy for everyone to achieve moksha because of the level of spirituality you must attain but Hindus believe that by living a good life – good dharma and karma that a person can achieve a better reincarnation and that through time and dedication everyone should fulfil their ultimate goal of liberation and becoming one with Brahman **AE6**

3. (a) • The word means path or yoke
- There are three: karma, jnana, bhakti
- Brief description of each is acceptable
- They are means of achieving moksha
- They all have strict moral codes
- Some have caste restrictions **KU3**

(b) • Dharma is duty
- Universal dharma – laws of nature
- Ashrama dharma – duties according to stage of life
- Varna dharma – duties according to social standing
- Sanctioned by the Vedas
- Sanctioned in the Gita **KU4**

(c) *It is important to note that candidates are not required to write eight different points in this answer.*
- Krishna lays great stress on doing your own dharma therefore it is more important to do dharma
- Failure to do dharma is bad karma – means you can't attain moksha
- Performing dharma is good karma – need good karma to achieve moksha
- Margas contain dharma so the two cannot be separated
- Overcoming avidya is more important than both
- Margas' focus is achieving moksha, dharma's focus is not
- Dharma concerned with maintaining order and getting good karma
- Krishna lays great stress on the margas, especially bhakti as a means to moksha
- Dharma is a goal of life like moksha, margas are the way of achieving moksha and performing dharma **AE8**

## SECTION 4: Islam

1. (a) • Freewill is a gift from Allah
   • It makes us unique in the whole of creation
   • Gives us freedom to behave how we want
   • We are also given Fitrah. This is the inner moral compass we all have. It steers us when we make decisions. We can respond to it or ignore it **KU3**

(b) *Maximum of two marks for each effect.*
   • It can result in suffering
   • We must learn what is and is not appropriate behaviour. Suffering that arises from the misuse of freewill is therefore a teaching tool
   • We are left with the decision of whether or not to repent
   • This allows us to show Allah we know we have made a mistake and shows we want to make up for it
   • It means we may be judged poorly by Allah
   • If we are not good khalifah (vice-regents) then the recording angels will mark down black dots in our Book of Life **AE6**

2. (a) *It is important to note that candidates are not required to write six different points in this answer.*
   • Reward for submission. Being close to Allah is better than all the possessions in earthly life
   • Paradise is promised for those who submit
   • Those who submit will be saved from Hell ('agony of the Fire')
   • Rewards for those who are patient and worship devoutly
   • Islam means submission
   • We have a duty to convey His Message to those who don't submit
   • If you follow Allah He will love you and forgive you for your wrongdoing
   • Submission is their goal during life
   • Taqwa and Ihsan **KU6**

(b) **Paradise**
   • Abiding place of the Righteous
   • An abode of bliss
   • Gardens with flowing rivers
   • Shade and fountains
   • No intense sun or cold
   • Milk and honey (protection and plenty)
   • Thrones, cushions, carpets, etc
   • Place of security. Protected from Hell

   **Hell**
   • An abyss
   • Heat of the sun
   • Falling to a great depth
   • Regret for evil done
   • Barbed fruits
   • Boiling water
   • Remedial nature **KU3**

(c) *It is important to note that candidates are not required to write six different points in this answer.*

   **Yes**
   • The Qur'an says that people who do not believe in Allah and obey Him will be punished in Hell.
   • Some traditions teach that after death you are questioned by an angel about Allah and if you answer you believe in Him you will immediately be taken to Paradise
   • Islam clearly teaches that life is a test to see if we are worthy of life in Paradise. Remaining faithful during the good and bad times means the recording angels will put white dots in our Book of Life
   • Observing the Pillars and living by Islamic law out of habit is not enough if you do not have the genuine faith behind it

   • The first Pillar is the statement of belief that Allah is the only God and Muhammad is His Messenger. It underpins all other Islamic teaching therefore it must be the key factor in securing a place in Paradise

   **No**
   • Having faith is not enough. It must also be backed up with good conduct, following Shariah law and observing the Five Pillars
   • Islam teaches that everyone will be resurrected on the Day of Judgement, therefore everyone will go on to have eternal life. However, it is only those who are faithful that will experience it in Paradise while others will experience it in Hell **AE6**

3. (a) • Approach salah with the right frame of mind
   • Wear appropriate clothing
   • Wash hands to wrist three times
   • Rinse mouth three times
   • Inhale water through nose and expel three times
   • Wash whole face three times
   • Wash arm from wrist to elbow three times
   • Wash over head and neck
   • Wash out ears
   • Wash feet
   • Wash ankles
   • Face Makkah **KU3**

(b) • To communicate with Allah
   • To remember Allah
   • To submit to Allah's will
   • To fulfil one of the five pillars
   • Reminds us that we are Allah's servants
   • Keeps us on the right path
   • Opportunity to thank Allah
   • Keeps religion a priority over everything else **KU4**

(c) *It is important to note that candidates are not required to write eight different points in this answer.*

   **Individual benefits:**
   • Leads to a divine reward
   • Organises an individual's time during the day
   • Spiritual benefits – joy of being in Allah's presence
   • Comfort in times of sorrow
   • Maintains an individual's faith

   **Community benefits:**
   • Focal point for the community
   • Friday prayers at the mosque allows fellowship
   • Brings a sense of community to the wider family of Islam
   • Reinforces bonds of brotherhood
   • Raises profile of the mosque as a community centre **AE8**

## SECTION 5: Judaism

1. (a) • The moral rules he has set down
   • The obedience he demands
   • The example set by the people of Israel to the world
   • Nothing happens without his permission
   • Nothing happens without his knowledge
   • The Jewish laws **KU3**

(b) *Maximum of two marks for each effect.*
   • Stray from righteous ways
   • Suffering occurs
   • Setting a poor example to the world
   • Impacts on the covenant
   • We become disobedient
   • We stray from the path God has set for us
   • His purposes cannot be achieved **AE6**

2. (a) *It is important to note that candidates are not required to write six different points in this answer.*
   - Sacred texts say little about the world to come
   - No one view agreed upon
   - Olam Ha-Ba
   - This world is a preparation for Olam Ha-Ba
   - Torah suggests that one is rejoining one's ancestors
   - Beliefs about Sheol
   - Soul continues to exist but not necessarily in a conscious state
   - Traditional Judaism accepts resurrection of the dead, Reform rejects the idea
   - Day of Judgement: righteous – eternal life, unrighteous Gehenna, 50/50 people to Gehenna and purified for return
   - Heaven (Gan Eden) – place of great joy and peace
   - Olam Heamet – life replayed **KU6**

   (b) - Time of freedom and peace for all
   - Involves a return to the Temple
   - An individual described as Messiah will lead the age
   - Biblical teaching e.g. ploughshares, messenger of peace, resurrection of the dead
   - Orthodox – belief that the Messiah is yet to come
   - Hasidic – coming of the Messiah is imminent
   - Progressive/Liberal/Reform – generally no belief that the Messiah is an individual more of a metaphor for a new age of peace and harmony
   - Line of David
   - Possibly an individual or a community
   - Conduct of mankind will determine arrival date of Messiah **KU4**

   (c) *It is important to note that candidates are not required to write six different points in this answer.* **AE6**

3. (a) - The word Torah includes both the Written and the Oral Law since they were both given to Moses on Mount Sinai
   - The Oral Law consists of explanations and interpretations of the Written Law and it was passed on by word of mouth
   - Moses passed on the Oral Law given at Mount Sinai to his successor, Joshua, who in turn passed it to his successor, in a chain that was carried on until the Oral Law was written down many centuries later **KU3**

   (b) - Contains the guidelines to Judaism
   - Torah means 'instructions' or 'teaching'
   - To help Jews to obey the goals: obey God and to build and maintain a relationship with Him
   - It covers in a whole way of life and Jews use it to study ethics, justice, religion and for education
   - Its study is central to Judaism and this is emphasised in the Ethics of the Fathers and in Jewish prayers **KU4**

   (c) *It is important to note that candidates are not required to write eight different points in this answer.*
   **YES**
   - Throughout time, new discoveries and social conditions have changed people's ways of living and thinking about the world we live in therefore the Oral Law made it possible for Jews to live by the Torah as new conditions arose
   - Moses received both the written and oral law therefore they are both relevant since through the oral law, God taught Moses how the commandments were to be kept
   - The oral laws are classified under specific headings and are related to the written law
   - Just as the Mishnah was an interpretation and development of the Written Law, so the Gemarah was a record of the further interpretations and discussions of the Mishnah over many centuries therefore they are both relevant

   - In addition to law, the oral Torah also contains a vast amount of material on all sorts of subjects such as medicine, social conditions, comments on events of the day and so on
   - Many rabbis wrote commentaries to guide people through it
   - It is not only a record of discussions but an entire social history
   - It is an ongoing process and is always based on the principles outlined in the Torah … this is why rulings continue to be added to the Halachah
   **NO**
   - The written Torah is all we need … the 10 commandments give all the religious and ethical guidance that are necessary to achieve the goals
   - Orthodox Jews take a very literal view of the written Torah
   - The rituals of worship, the celebration of festivals and the rules for everyday living must remain the same throughout history. Orthodox Jews believe that it is wrong to allow historical events and social changes to influence the interpretation of God's word **AE8**

## SECTION 6: Sikhism

1. (a) - All humans have a dual nature – a physical body which is part of God's creation and a spiritual soul (atman) which is part of God
   - The atman is immortal and was part of God before the universe was created
   - The atman is on a journey which will take a person through many life times towards reunion with God
   - Sikhs can choose to either follow God's Will and be open to God's Grace or they can choose to ignore it and concentrate on themselves, haumai, this will take them away from reunion with God and they will become stuck on the cycle of birth, death and rebirth. People who are totally self-centred and separated from God are called Manmukh
   - By using your freewill to turn away from God you will create Maya or illusion and this will also separate you from God **KU3**

   (b) *Maximum of two marks for each effect.*
   - Leads to haumai – self-centredness which means a person is not open to God's Grace or God's Will which therefore means that they literally forget their goal of obtaining reunion with God because they are too busy fulfilling their own needs and desires
   - People will also fail to see the reality of their situation and therefore suffer from Maya – a mistaken belief that material things are more important than spiritual reunion with God
   - This means that humans create their own barrier to reunion which in turn means that they are stuck on the cycle of birth, death and rebirth **AE6**

2. (a) *It is important to note that candidates are not required to write six different points in this answer.*
   - Devotion to God
   - Worship God
   - Prayer
   - Nam Simran
   - Perform dharma
   - Detachment
   - Ethical behaviour **KU6**

   (b) - Can take place when a human is living – someone who had reunion with God is known as jivan mukht
   - Person is believed to be in a state of unending bliss and is now free from endless cycle of rebirth

- When a person dies they are no longer reborn in human form but will remain permanently with God who is pure spirit
- "...emotional attachment is eradicated; all my enemies are eliminated. He is always ever-present, here and now, watching over me..." (GGS 1000) **KU4**

(c) *It is important to note that candidates are not required to write six different points in this answer.*
- Jivan Muhkti can't be described so it can't be realistic
- Cannot explain the joy so people are aspiring to something they will have difficulty knowing
- Recognition of maya goes against instincts – very difficult thing to do
- Blinded by our own self-centredness so we would find it very difficult to achieve reunion
- Living a good life can bring you closer to God and hence reunion
- The ego gets in the way of reunion with God so by serving others the influence of the ego declines and chances of reunion increase
- More realistic not to separate the two – Kirt Kana and Vand Chhanka lead to closeness with God
- Nam japna is the foundation of life
- Five Vices even make living a good life very difficult **AE6**

3. (a) 
- He was the first prophet of the Sikh faith
- The first human guru
- The founder of the Sikh religion – he began his public mission after a revelation from God
- Guru Nanak emphasised the belief that all human beings are equal and could reunite with God in this present life cycle by continually turning their hearts and mind to Him
- Guru Nanak was a leader and a role model to the Sikhs
- Nanak composed hymns which are still used today to teach people about God and his Will **KU3**

(b) 
- Extreme care and attention is given to a copy of the Guru Granth Sahib – it is treated with the same respect you would give to a living, human teacher
- Always given a place of central importance
- Always kept raised off the ground and kept clean
- Carried out of a special room used only for the Granth and brought with respect in a ceremonial procession into the prayer hall. Daily ceremony known as Parkash Karna
- People bring offerings to the Granth and these are used to help the daily running of the Gurdwara
- All worshippers will bow before the Granth when they enter the prayer hall and will sit on the floor below the level of the Guru Granth Sahib as a sign of their respect as well as a sign of their belief that all are equal before God **KU4**

(c) *It is important to note that candidates are not required to write eight different points in this answer.*
- Guru Nanak laid down the "foundations" of the Sikh faith and showed how Sikhs can live in harmony with God's Will
- It was through Guru Nanak's revelation from God that Sikhism began, so this places him in a unique position
- However, a Sikh must realise that they cannot achieve reunion with God on their own, they need help in order to do this
- Help comes from God's Grace but also from the Ten Human Gurus not Guru Nanak alone
- In addition to this the Guru Granth Sahib is also described as a living Guru and inspires, communicates knowledge in exactly the same way as a human Guru would
- Sikhs would therefore not see any differentiation between the Ten Living Gurus, Nanak being one of them and the Guru Granth Sahib

- The Gurus are all required to give guidance to a Sikh as it is the Guru's words and "virtues" that are needed as a guide if reunion is to be achieved
- The balance is achieved because all the Guru's words are the Word of God or Shabad **AE8**

## RM&PS HIGHER
## PAPER 1
## 2010

**Weighting of questions:**
*Knowledge and Understanding – approximately 50% of total marks available. The generic requirement for KU is that accurate, relevant and detailed knowledge of content is demonstrated; the information is presented in a coherent manner and information is communicated effectively using accurate terminology.*

*Analysis and Evaluation – approximately 50% of total marks available. The generic requirement for AE is for analysis of concepts, processes, evidence etc to be shown and evaluation to be balanced and informed.*

*No marks will be awarded where candidates simply provide a list. Any terms listed must be accompanied by a brief explanation to gain a mark. The bullet points under the heading of "examples of area covered" is a general guide as to the area that candidates may discuss in their answers. The examples are neither mandatory nor exhaustive.*

## SECTION 1

1. (a) *Each basis of religious morality should be accompanied by an explanation to gain a mark. Examples of areas covered:*
   - Sacred writings
   - Faith
   - Tradition
   - Reason
   - Religious experience
   - Examples from each of these will be given credit
   
   **KU4**

   (b) *Each feature should be accompanied by an explanation to gain a mark. Examples of areas covered:*
   - Consequentialist
   - Bentham and Mill developed key ideas
   - Based on idea of greatest happiness for greatest number
   - Act Utilitarianism
   - Rule Utilitarianism       **KU4**

   (c) *Examples of areas covered:*
   - Equal opportunities: in education and employment for example
   - Media Stereotyping: male and female stereotyping in all forms of the media
   - The Family: roles of men and women at home       **KU4**

   (d) *Each point should be accompanied by an explanation to gain a mark. Examples of areas covered:*
   - Equal access to education and employment regardless of gender
   - No discrimination because of gender
   - Relates to disability and ethnicity       **KU2**

   (e) *Answers may vary depending on the religious perspective adopted. Examples of areas covered:*
   **Equal Opportunities**
   - Concern that traditional roles are being undermined by equal opportunities
   - Concern that traditional roles may remain in spite of equal opportunities legislation
   - Created equal by God
   - Created with different roles by God
   - Concern that equality is not being promoted enough

   **Stereotyping**
   - Inaccurate thus leading to discrimination
   - Women perceived as sex objects
   - Men perceived as sexual predators
   - Concern that not enough is being done to stop stereotyping

   **Family**
   - Breakdown of the family because neither fulfil a family role
   - Equal roles should be in the family
   - Family is where divinely ordained roles should be enacted       **AE6**

   (f) *Responses can be specific or general in which two headings of response type are used. The UN is used as an example below:*

   *Examples of areas covered:*
   UN urged that governments tackle the following:
   - CEDAW
   - Beijing Platform for Action
   - The persistent and increasing burden of poverty on women
   - Inequalities and inadequacies in and unequal access to education and training
   - Inequalities and inadequacies in and unequal access to health care and related services
   - Violence against women
   - The effects of armed or other kinds of conflict on women, including those living under foreign occupation
   - Inequality in economic structures and policies, in all forms of productive activities and in access to resources
   - Inequality between men and women in the sharing of power and decision-making at all levels
   - Insufficient mechanisms at all levels to promote the advancement of women
   - Lack of respect for and inadequate promotion and protection of the human rights of women
   - Stereotyping of women and inequality in women's access to and participation in all communication systems, especially in the media
   - Gender inequalities in the management of natural resources and in the safeguarding of the environment   **KU4**

   (g) *A wide variety of answers is possible to this question. Candidates are not expected to write six separate points but may do so if they wish. Ideally candidates will write two-three points with expansion. Responses to UN action is used as an example below.*

   *Examples of areas covered:*
   **Agree**
   - Many countries have policies to address issues noted above
   - People are aware of the issues raised above
   - Statistical evidence of improvement
   - Financial support to poor countries trying to implement policies of equality

   **Disagree**
   - Compliance is patchy
   - Progress is slow
   - Corruption is rife
   - Traditional views still strong in some countries
   - Brought it out into the open, changed little because it still goes on.       **AE6**

   (h) *Each feature should be accompanied by an explanation to gain a mark. Examples of areas covered:*
   - Involves human reason
   - Involves performing one's duty
   - The Categorical Imperative
   - Respect for persons       **KU3**

   (i) *Candidates are not expected to write eight separate points but may do so if they wish. Ideally candidates should make two or three points with expansion.*

   *Examples of areas covered:*
   - Respect for persons includes treating everyone equally - women in developing world should get equal access to education, health etc

- Respect for life prohibits infanticide and acts of violence in Kantian ethics
- Principles of equality and respect should be paramount not the consequences
- Reason dictates that full development of individuals would benefit society
- Kant had an ambiguous approach to women which may have a negative impact on the intellectual status of women in the developing world
- Kantian maxims would promote education of all women
- Kantian maxims would protect women from the excesses of violence and sex **AE8**

2. (a) *Each basis of religious morality should be accompanied by an explanation to gain a mark. Examples of areas covered:*
   - Sacred writings
   - Faith
   - Tradition
   - Reason
   - Religious experience
   - Examples from each of these will be given credit **KU4**

   (b) *Each feature should be accompanied by an explanation to gain a mark. Examples of areas covered:*
   - Consequentialist
   - Bentham and Mill developed key ideas
   - Based on idea of greatest happiness for greatest number
   - Act Utilitarianism
   - Rule Utilitarianism **KU4**

   (c) *Examples of areas covered:*
   - Poverty: most crime committed in areas where there is poor housing and unemployment
   - Family: criminal families, poor parenting skills
   - Environment: deprived area which fosters low self esteem
   - Psychological: individuals may have a criminal disposition **KU4**

   (d) *Each point should be accompanied by an explanation to gain a mark. Examples of areas covered:*
   - Prisoner does not re-offend
   - Prisoner learns the error of his or her ways
   - Prisoner is supported during incarceration
   - Prisoner changes into a law abiding citizen **KU2**

   (e) *Answers may vary depending on the religious perspective adopted. Examples of areas covered:*
   - Family is central to religious values eg respect for parents
   - Golden Rule: do unto others etc
   - Religious moral precepts eg 10 commandments
   - Injustice/Inequality: a concern because we are all equal in God's eyes and some may be denied equality thus committing crime
   - Human rights: denial of human rights of perpetrator and victim
   - Respect for persons: crime may result from a lack of respect for self and others
   - Compassion: religions generally are on the side of the less fortunate - a concern because there is a calling to help
   - Breaking of commandments **AE6**

   (f) *Examples of areas that may be covered:*
   - Hanging: legs and arms bound together, rope around neck, snaps vertebrae.
   - Lethal Injection: strapped to gurney, three lines inserted, unconsciousness followed by paralysis and death
   - Firing Squad: varies, certain number of in squad, target on heart, sandbags behind prisoner, all aim for heart
   - Gassing: strapped to chair, cyanide crystals dropped, instructed to inhale to hasten death
   - Electrocution: strapped to chair, electrodes attached, bursts of electricity continued until death **KU4**

   (g) *Candidates are not expected to write six separate points but may do so if they wish. Ideally candidates will write two-three points with expansion. Responses to UN action is used as an example below. Examples of areas covered:*
   **Agree**
   - Protection: public protected from criminals
   - Deterrence: puts others off committing serious crimes
   - Justice: justice is seen to be done
   - Financial: the convict is no longer a burden on society
   - Life for a life

   **Disagree**
   - No deterrence: people still commit serious crimes where it exists
   - Protection: public only protected from executed criminal, but other criminals exist
   - State sanctioned murder- state lowers itself to the level of the murderer.
   - Innocents executed **AE6**

   (h) *Each feature should be accompanied by an explanation to gain a mark.*
   - Involves human reason
   - Involves performing one's duty
   - The Categorical Imperative
   - Respect for persons **KU3**

   (i) *Candidates are not expected to write eight separate points but may do so if they wish. Ideally candidates should make two or three points with expansion.*

   *Examples of areas covered:*
   - Offender should be punished because he deserves it
   - Justice and righteous are basis of human value and dignity
   - Kant has universal view of morality, and murder is ultimate infringement so … can't allow murderer to live
   - Justice must be seen to be done
   - Justice would cease to be justice if it were bartered away for any consideration whatsoever
   - Categorically obliged to apply law. Failure to punish with death penalty is like saying that murder is ok **AE8**

3. (a) *Each basis of religious morality should be accompanied by an explanation to gain a mark.*

   *Examples of areas covered:*
   - Sacred writings
   - Faith
   - Tradition
   - Reason
   - Religious experience
   - Examples from each of these will be given credit **KU4**

   (b) *Each feature should be accompanied by an explanation to gain a mark. Examples of areas covered:*
   - Consequentialist
   - Bentham and Mill developed key ideas
   - Based on idea of greatest happiness for greatest number
   - Act Utilitarianism
   - Rule Utilitarianism **KU3**

   (c) *Examples of areas covered:*
   - Poor resources
   - Corruption
   - War
   - Trading inequalities
   - Poor education
   - Poor health **KU4**

   (d) *Each point should be accompanied by an explanation to gain a mark. Examples of areas covered:*
   - Fair trade
   - Education
   - Equal distribution of resources

- Democracy
- Military aid to support unstable governments
- Cancellation of debt                                    **KU2**

(e) *Answers may vary depending on the religious perspective adopted. Examples of areas covered:*
- Duty of care to the less fortunate
- Abuse of power by corrupt leaders
- Unfair trading arrangements between developed and developing nations
- Against God's will
- Poor stewardship of God-given resources
- Complacency of developed world in dealing with poverty                                                    **AE6**

(f) *Examples of areas covered:*
- Agreements on conventions relating to various emissions
- International summits of world leaders
- Target setting for reductions in various emissions
- Aware raising in home nations
- Action in home nations
- "Crying foul" when conventions are broken especially by major powers.                                    **KU4**

(g) *A wide variety of answers is possible to this question. Candidates are not expected to write six separate points but may do so if they wish. Ideally candidates will write two-three points with expansion. Responses to UN action is used as an example below. Examples of areas covered:*

**Agree**
- Efforts being made to reduce the problem
- Unprecedented awareness of the issue
- Greater sense of urgency to deal with the crisis
- The public are prepared to make sacrifices to save the planet
- Major investment into global warming initiatives

**Disagree**
- Progress is slow
- Major players reluctant to participate
- Cost puts major industries off
- Fossil fuel demand and consumption is as high as ever   **AE6**

(h) *Each feature should be accompanied by an explanation to gain a mark.*
- Involves human reason
- Involves performing one's duty
- The Categorical Imperative
- Respect for persons                                      **KU3**

(i) *Candidates are not expected to write eight separate points but may do so if they wish. Ideally candidates should make two or three points with expansion.*

*Examples of areas covered:*
- Kant himself did not have a positive view of the environment – only rational beings are considered of moral worth
- Natural world's duty is to serve human beings thus global warming is not an issue
- Without humans the natural world has no purpose
- Kant did not have the awareness we have of the environment
- Kant believed in the beauty of nature - could be expanded to include its intricacy for which we have a responsibility to maintain
- Kantian ethics speaks of the intrinsic value of things we now know the intrinsic value of the environment thus have a duty to protect it
- Causes of global warming may involve using people as a means to an end eg industrial pollution caused by consumerism
- Means to an end principle could be applied to global warming

- As moral beings we have duties, perhaps one of these is to care for the environment
- Maxims- reason tell us that exploitation of the environment for this generation cannot be right if other generations are to suffer                            **AE8**

4. (a) *Each basis of religious morality should be accompanied by an explanation to gain a mark. Examples of areas covered:*
- Sacred writings
- Faith
- Tradition
- Reason
- Religious experience
- Examples from each of these will be given credit   **KU4**

(b) *Each feature should be accompanied by an explanation to gain a mark. Examples of areas covered:*
- Consequentialist
- Bentham and Mill developed key ideas
- Based on idea of greatest happiness for greatest number
- Act Utilitarianism
- Rule Utilitarianism                                      **KU3**

(c) *Examples of areas covered:*
- IVF
- Research
- Pre-implantation genetic diagnosis
- Pre-implantation genetic selection
- Saviour siblings                                         **KU4**

(d) *Each point should be accompanied by an explanation to gain a mark. Examples of areas covered:*
- Regulations about storage
- Licensing of clinics
- Applications for embryo research
- Monitoring of clinics
- Statutory body to oversee use of embryos               **KU2**

(e) *Answers may vary depending on the religious perspective adopted. Examples of areas covered:*
- Beginning of life
- Rights of the embryo
- Personhood of embryo
- Spiritual status
- Breaks natural law
- Slippery slope towards eugenics
- The purpose of their use
- Interference with God's will                            **AE6**

(f) *Examples of areas covered:*
- Patient in a coma and unable to choose
- Medical staff unable to consult with patient or relatives
- Patient in extreme suffering- use of double effect
- Cost effectiveness                                       **KU4**

(g) *Candidates are not expected to write six separate points but may do so if they wish. Ideally candidates will write two-three points with expansion. Responses to UN action is used as an example below. Examples of areas covered:*

**Agree**
- Reduces suffering
- Better use of resources
- Saves money
- Reduces burden on families
- Allows death with dignity

**Disagree**
- Human rights issues for patients and medical staff
- Legal issues
- Places a financial value on life
- Opportunity for abuse
- Against God's will/command                              **AE6**

(h) *Each feature should be accompanied by an explanation to gain a mark.*
- Involves human reason
- Involves performing one's duty
- The Categorical Imperative
- Respect for persons                                  **KU3**

(i) *Candidates are not expected to write eight separate points but may do so if they wish. Ideally candidates should make two or three points with expansion. Examples of areas covered:*
- If sanctity of life is a universal maxim then destroying life is wrong
- Kantian ethics teaches respect for the person, euthanasia shows disrespect because it is taken away
- If one terminally ill person could be euthanized then all borderline life is under threat
- Respect for life is important in Kantian ethics so if dying individuals are treated as a burden, respect for life is diminished
- Euthanasia could be used as treating people as a means to an end eg removal of burden, reduction of cost
- If it is right to euthanize one person then it should be euthanize all- reason dictates that this is clearly a rule that cannot be universalized
- Kantian ethics teaches respect for persons – dying person in a coma is no longer a sentient being, therefore can be put to sleep
- Kantian ethics has no interest in consequences – therefore possible drawbacks of euthanasia are irrelevant     **AE8**

5. (a) *Each basis of religious morality should be accompanied by an explanation to gain a mark. Examples of areas covered:*
- Sacred writings
- Faith
- Tradition
- Reason
- Religious experience                                 **KU4**

(b) *Each feature should be accompanied by an explanation to gain a mark. Examples of areas covered:*
- Consequentialist
- Bentham and Mill developed key ideas
- Based on idea of greatest happiness for greatest number
- Act Utilitarianism
- Rule Utilitarianism                                  **KU3**

(c) *Examples of areas covered:*
- Self Defence: defend your country in the event of an attack
- Territory: defend/attack territory which has resource or security interests
- Imperial: attack country to expand empire
- Pre-emptive strike: attack before they attack you
- Failed diplomacy: non violent means of resolving the dispute fail                                         **KU4**

(d) *Each point should be accompanied by an explanation to gain a mark. Examples of areas covered:*
- May be absolutist and have nothing to do with war
- May be alternativist and refuse to fight but perform other activities eg help in kitchens or medical wings
- May give definitions of different extent of pacifist beliefs eg principle, pragmatic, selective
- May participate in demonstrations, marches, sign petitions etc                                          **KU2**

(e) *Answers may vary depending on the religious perspective adopted. Examples of areas covered:*
- Against some religious teachings in sacred books
- Failure to find peaceful resolution to the problem
- War always leads to death and destruction no matter what the reason

- Greed underlies most of the reasons
- Power underlies most of the reasons
- War always leads to death and life is sacred/special. No reason can justify the taking of life because of this.
- Goes against religious teachings eg 'Turn the other cheek'
- Goes against the example of religious leaders eg pacifist strategies of Gandhi and Martin Luther King
- Doesn't fulfil our responsibility to look after the world
- For some religions killing could be hurting part of God (Quakers)
- Taking life could be seen as playing God        **AE6**

(f) *Examples of areas covered:*
- Human cost: instant death for those at the centre, maiming of those further away
- Infrastructure: utilities destroyed
- Environment: flora and fauna destroyed, land polluted
- Huge loss of life:
- Immediate deaths and future ones due to radiation
- Environmental damage:
- Damage the ozone layer. This would damage crops and increase skin cancer cases.
- Nuclear winter would lead to drops in temperature. This would destroy crops leading to widespread starvation.
- Electromagnetic Pulse (EMP) would knock out all communication systems (TVs, radios, computers, telephones, power grids)                        **KU4**

(g) *Candidates are not expected to write six separate points but may do so if they wish. Ideally candidates will write two-three points with expansion. Responses to UN action is used as an example below. Examples of areas covered:*

**Agree**
- Effective deterrent. Enemies are less likely to attack if you possess them
- Cost effective. Less manpower is required so it reduces cost of employing lots of service personnel
- Fewer losses of servicemen. More lives would be lost fighting a conventional ground war than launching nuclear weapons from a distance
- Unstable world. More countries are starting to develop them. Need the capacity to act against unpredictable situations in the world's trouble spots
- No more morally questionable than other weapons. Killing is killing. Nuclear weapons would end war quickly, avoiding more suffering
- They cannot be un-invented. Making sure others don't use them to destroy or blackmail people is more likely if you possess them

**Disagree**
- The use or threatened use of nuclear weapons, which could destroy everyone creates a great deal of fear which is morally wrong.
- The more countries with nuclear capabilities the greater the danger of nuclear war breaking out.
- Danger of accidental nuclear explosions.
- Increased possibility of environmental pollution from nuclear manufacturing plants.
- Nuclear weapons are very expensive. The money spent on them could be better spent in dealing with all the human and social problems of the world.
- They don't work as a deterrent. The threat of violent retaliation usually makes the enemy more determined to win.                                                 **AE6**

(h) *Each feature should be accompanied by an explanation to gain a mark.*
- Involves human reason
- Involves performing one's duty

- The Categorical Imperative
- Respect for persons **KU3**

(i) *Candidates are not expected to write eight separate points but may do so if they wish. Ideally candidates should make two or three points with expansion.*

*Examples of areas covered:*
- War has a human cost – treating people as a means to an end
- Kant wanted a perfect society – death and destruction caused by modern armamentsis not a part of that society
- Reason tells us that WMD should be avoided
- Destruction of war- reason tells us that we should avoid that
- Not possible to universalise all the reasons for going to war
- Can permission to kill be universalised?
- Universal law – is war always is wrong? No, so wars must be right
- Duty is to protect life
- Duty is to preserve freedom and democracy so war is acceptable
- Can we have peace and happiness whilst others do not – duty to fight for this for all people
- Is 'do not murder' a universal law? This would mean using weapons is always wrong (categorical imperative)
- Modern armaments involve the death of the innocent therefore it is to be avoided
- War is wrong because it punishes without justification.
- You could argue your duty is to protect the freedom and values of your society. You may need to use weapons for this to be protected
- Reason would tell us people should live in a country where people have their human rights upheld. We have a moral duty to fight against dictators who abuse people's human rights
- Kant wanted a perfect society. Sometimes you have to fight for peace in the long-term eg WWII
- If you do not stop an aggressor it may lead to more problems in the long-term. They could invade weaker nations. Reason and duty would tell you to intervene to stop such exploitation
- Highest good (summum bonnum). You may have peace and happiness but are you worthy of this if others are denied it and you have the ability to do something? We ought to fight for them
- Kant said instinct should be ignored over duty – what you ought to do. We may want to be pacifist, knowing the devastating effects of weapons, but it may be our duty to defend our country or our allies **AE8**

# SECTION 2

(a) *Examples of areas covered:*
- Follows a four stage process of Observation, Hypothesis, Experiment, Verification
- A process to study the natural world and much of what it contains, in a systematic way
- It is based on evidence and experiment
- It focuses on the desire to challenge and evaluate all truth claims
- It presupposes that the world is intelligible and orderly
- It aims to put nature to the test
- It uses the processes of induction, deduction and verification
- Provides data which can be independently tested by other scientists
- Provides evidence/information of a provisional nature which is subject to change in the light of new evidence/discoveries **KU4**

(b) *Examples of areas covered:*
- It is God's way of communicating with us
- Supernatural act of self-communication
- It contains the truth … it reveals the purpose of creation
- Revelation through Scripture (the word of God) … Special Revelation (Revelatio Verbalis) … rooted in God's plan to redeem us … is addressed to man as a sinner and can be understood by faith
- Revelation through Nature (the works of God) … General Revelation (Revelatio Realis) … rooted in creation and addressed to human reason
- Through revelation God reveals what is hidden or partially hidden
- It is infallible because it cannot be proven false by scientific means
- The supreme revelation of God is through Christ
- Theology (the study of God) would be impossible without a self-revelation of God
- God takes the initiative in revealing something of himself to us **KU4**

(c) *Examples of areas covered:*
- The sense of meaning, value and purpose in human life is provided by religion and is often related to the concept of God or other spiritual aspects so religion is necessary to do this
- We also need a set of moral values/principles to live by … science cannot give us this as it is not in this 'business'
- Issues which are beyond the scope of science eg beliefs about good and evil, existential questions, the question of God … are not scientific
- Religion is concerned with aspects of reality which aim to relate to why things are as they are eg the significance of human consciousness, transcendence, the intelligibility of the world etc
- Religion operates at the personal, individual, subjective level and not with the universal … as science does … therefore it is much more meaningful
- If you add religious beliefs and values to scientific ideas you can get a much more complete picture than just science on its own
- Scientific bias not always objective
- Falsifiability – scientific statements are tentative **AE6**

(d) *Examples of areas covered:*
- The universe itself is the most vital piece of evidence for the existence of God. If God does not exist the world as we know it cannot be explained
- Everything that moves is moved by something else. This cannot be infinite or the movement would not have started in the first place. There must be an 'unmoved mover' – God
- Everything has a cause. There cannot be an infinite number of causes therefore there must be an 'uncaused cause' – God is the First Cause
- Nothing can come from nothing. Something only comes into existence as a result of something that already exists. There must be some 'necessary being' that exists of itself – God.
- If you then consider the universe, you can follow the same logical argument until you get to a stage of the First Cause of the universe as well
- This First Cause of the universe has not been caused by anything else so must be the ultimate First Cause. This is what we mean by God. **KU4**

(e) *Examples of areas covered:*
- There does not have to be a First/final Cause to the universe – it might have come into existence spontaneously with no actual/first cause
- The First Cause of the universe may not be God … it may be a natural event

- If everything has a cause, then God must be caused by something, you cannot just stop at any point in the chain and randomly call this God
- Just because individual things within the universe have causes, it does not mean that the world/universe itself has a cause
- Just because every human being has a mother it does not follow that the universe has a mother
- This is too simplistic an argument … God is far greater than we can ever explain with our finite logic.
- Hume's criticisms
- Kant's criticisms                                        **AE4**

(f) *Examples of areas covered:*
- God created the world over a period of time … Timescale varies between Genesis 1 and 2 … human beings were created as the final part/climax of creation over 6 days
- In Genesis 1, human beings are created last after all plant and animal life
- In Genesis 1, male and female are created together
- In Genesis 2, the humans are created first and other life forms follow. The man is created first and the woman is created from the man's rib
- In Genesis 2, God took some soil from the ground and breathed life into the man who became a living being
- Origin of life is as per evolutionary theory          **KU4**

(g) *Examples of areas covered:*
- Life began with simple single-celled creatures
- By chance they mutated and developed into more complex life forms
- Species develop and adapt to their environment
- Life has developed over many millions of years
- All forms of life originate from the same beginnings so life has a common source
- Extinction and hereditary
- Survival of the fittest
- Natural selection                                       **KU4**

(h) *It is important to note that candidates are not required to write ten different points in this answer. Credit should be given where candidates have expanded upon the points they have made. Examples of areas covered:*
**Unjustified**
- Evolution theory is convincing
- Evolution provides good evidence to support this whereas there is no comparable evidence for the existence of God
- Science gives us a much better understanding as it is based on facts, evidence, observations and not just on belief or speculation about God as creator
- Evolution theory suggests a spontaneous 'explosion' based on natural laws so there is no need to suggest any other … unnecessary … power like God to explain it
- The idea of God was only necessary when we did not know enough about how the universe came into existence – before the development of other theories
- It is foolish to believe in a God whose existence cannot be proved
- Complexity can be explained naturally
- At best all that can be said is that it was designed, can't say that it was the Christian God

**Justified**
- Fine tuning- has to be some kind of creative power behind universe ie God
- The universe needs some kind of final explanation – it is too complex to simply be the result of chance
- The presence of conscious, intelligent life in the universe suggests that there is a conscious 'mind' behind it all
- God gives it meaning and purpose

- It seems reasonable to believe that the Universe must have some kind of explanation or reasons for its existence even though this cannot be proved
- God is worshipped as creator by people of all religions.
- There are many things in life that people believe in which cannot be proved- scientifically or otherwise. If these are not seen as foolish, why pick out God as being any different?
- People have freedom to believe what they want without proof
**AE10**

*No marks will be awarded where candidates simply provide a list. Any terms listed must be accompanied by a brief explanation to gain a mark. The bullet points under the heading of "examples of areas covered" is a general guide as to the areas that candidates may discuss in their answers. The examples are neither mandatory nor exhaustive. NB Where candidates refer to appropriate sacred writings credit will be given. As a general guide a relevant and appropriate reference (which can be paraphrased or verbatim) will gain one mark. Where it is clearly applied to a concept or point it will receive a further mark. There is no limit on the number of references that can be used in an answer. However, relevance and appropriateness are essential.*

## SECTION 1: Buddhism

(a) *It is important to note that candidates are not required to write four different points in this answer. Credit should be given where candidates have expanded upon the points they have made.*

*Examples of areas covered:*
- 1st Noble Truth – the truth of suffering
- Translated as suffering, but has deeper philosophical meaning – unsatisfactoriness
- One of 3 marks of existence along with Anicca and Anatta
- All are true and Dukkha is unavoidable
- Suffering is at the heart of things – is inevitable in all aspects of life
  Many different kinds of suffering – emotional, physical etc    **KU4**

(b) *It is important to note that candidates are not required to write four different points in this answer. Credit should be given where candidates have expanded upon the points they have made.*

*Examples of areas covered:*
- Dukkha is a consequence of anicca
- Acceptance of anatta is a pre-requisite to reducing dukkha
- Dukkha is a feature of rebirth and determines rebirth
- Tanha causes dukkha    **AE4**

(c) *It is important to note that candidates are not required to write four different points in this answer. Credit should be given where candidates have expanded upon the points they have made.*

*Examples of areas covered:*
- Worldwide community of Buddhists
- Mainly understood as the community of monks
- Established by Buddha
- Life of devotion to Buddhist ideals
- Role of the Sangha in different Buddhist traditions
- Relationship between the Sangha and lay people    **KU4**

(d) *It is important to note that candidates are not required to write eight different points in this answer. Credit should be given where candidates have expanded upon the points they have made.*

*Examples of areas covered:*
**Agree**
- Sangha is about personal enlightenment
- Laity are a means to an end for the Sangha
- In some contexts the community exists for the benefit of the Sangha

**Disagree**
- Laity gain good karma by supporting the Sangha
- Sangha leads the people in religious devotion
- Sangha provides education
- Maintains traditions
- Provides social support for the laity    **AE8**

(e) *It is important to note that candidates are not required to write six different points in this answer. Credit should be given where candidates have expanded upon the points they have made.*

*Examples of areas covered:*
- Right speech
- Right conduct
- Right livelihood
- Golden rule
- Non harm
- No killing
- Compassion    **KU6**

(f) *It is important to note that candidates are not required to write six different points in this answer. Credit should be given where candidates have expanded upon the points they have made.*

*Examples of areas covered:*
- Concentration that leads to Enlightenment
- Samatha
- Vissapana
- Meta Bhavana    **KU6**

(g) *It is important to note that candidates are not required to write eight different points in this answer. Credit should be given where candidates have expanded upon the points they have made. Candidates may score a maximum of four marks for one response. Candidates may take an approach other than agreement and disagreement with the statement.*

*Examples of approaches:*
**Agree** (possibly a Mahayanist view)
- Morality (sila) is an important part of the Eightfold Path
- Sila is made up of right speech, conduct and livelihood – all connected
- All have to be observed to achieve Enlightenment
- Living a moral life is important because it means not harming others
- Good moral actions lead to a better rebirth
- Especially important to lay Buddhists who cannot practice meditation

**Disagree** (possibly a Theravadin view)
- Meditation more important – mind becomes skilled in seeing the universe as it is
- Purifies the mind
- Eightfold Path has three steps related to meditation
- Gets rid of the Three Poisons which are obstacles to enlightenment
- Enlightenment requires skilled mind and skilled actions
- Necessary for Buddha to achieve enlightenment, must be most important    **AE8**

## SECTION 2: Christianity

(a) *It is important to note that candidates are not required to write four different points in this answer. Credit should be given where candidates have expanded upon the points they have made.*

*Examples of areas covered:*
- Disobedience towards God
- Turning away from God
- Using freewill to disobey God
- Alienation from God
- Doing wrong
- Failing to follow God's commands    **KU4**

(b) *It is important to note that candidates are not required to write four different points in this answer. Credit should be given where candidates have expanded upon the points they have made.*

*Examples of areas covered*
- Act of sin leads to suffering
- Act of sin leads to alienation from God
- Act of sin leads to death

- Act of sin leads to breakdown of relationships with ourselves, natural world and each other
- Act of sin brings evil into the world
- Humanity alone cannot restore this damaged relationship
- For Christians, Christ through his death and resurrection can restore this relationship – healing atonement role of Christ

**AE4**

(c) *It is important to note that candidates are not required to write four different points in this answer. Credit should be given where candidates have expanded upon the points they have made.*

*Examples of areas covered:*
- Death in agony on cross
- Body removed by followers, wrapped and taken to tomb
- Followers visited tomb to care for body
- Body was not there
- Women spoken to Jesus
- Appearances to followers
- Ascent to Heaven
- Christ seen in the flesh by others **KU4**

(d) *It is important to note that candidates are not required to write eight different points in this answer. Credit should be given where candidates have expanded upon the points they have made. Candidates should not receive marks for KU used in question (c). Where new KU is introduced and used to make an AE point a mark should be awarded.*

*Examples of areas covered:*
**Agree**
- Much depends on one's beliefs about salvation
- Belief in the Resurrection and what it achieved are fundamental to the Christian life
- Resurrection demands that you are 'born again' in Jesus Christ
- To believe in the Resurrection but not in the moral life Jesus demanded is incompatible with Jesus' teaching
- Jesus required his disciples to be 'fishers of men' showing that Resurrection belief alone was insufficient

**Disagree**
- Some beliefs in predestination may suggest that God's will is more important than your personal beliefs in terms of salvation which is part of the Christian life
- If there is no belief in the Resurrection then there is no point in living a Christian life
- The resurrection is a key part of most creeds – morality does not have the same emphasis **AE8**

(e) *It is important to note that candidates are not required to write six different points in this answer. Credit should be given where candidates have expanded upon the points they have made.*

*Examples of areas covered:*
- Talking to God
- Following the example of Jesus when he spoke to God
- Form/part of worship
- Petitionary prayer- opportunity to ask for God's support
- Intecessionary prayer- opportunity to ask for others
- Quiet time with God
- Opportunity to meditate on beliefs, practices and teaching
- Main means of communicating with God
- Used for adoration
- Solitary/collective worship **KU6**

(f) *It is important to note that candidates are not required to write six different points in this answer. Credit should be given where candidates have expanded upon the points they have made.*

*Examples of areas covered:*
**Worship**
- Regular meetings to learn about and praise God/Jesus
- Participation in the sacraments as commanded by Jesus

**Witness**
- Spreading the Gospel of Jesus
- Standing up for beliefs when required

**Social Action**
- Lobbying
- Practical help- use of time and talents
- Standing up for what is right
- Working with the oppressed etc **KU6**

(g) *It is important to note that candidates are not required to write eight different points in this answer. Credit should be given where candidates have expanded upon the points they have made. Candidates may score a maximum of four marks for one response. Candidates may take an approach other than agreement and disagreement with the statement. Examples of approaches:*
**Agree**
- Prayer is talk – depends on action to make it work
- Action changes lives rather than waits for it to happen
- Action has a higher profile than prayer therefore it is a more effective advert for the Church
- Action brings direct tangible benefits to individuals, prayer is more subtle
- We live in a quick fix society today so prayer is too subtle – frontline action is more conspicuous
- Prayer never filled empty stomachs or healed broken limbs

**Disagree**
- Prayer makes the actions possible
- Prayer is the driving force behind Christian action
- Prayer leads Christians to an understanding of what social action they must take
- Prayer brings comfort and solace to the sad and defeated
- Prayer inspires to practical action and answers to prayers inspire even more **AE8**

# SECTION 3: Hinduism

(a) *It is important to note that candidates are not required to write four different points in this answer. Credit should be given where candidates have expanded upon the points they have made.*
*Examples of areas covered:*
- Nothing lasts
- The universe is impermanent
- The gods are impermanent
- The natural world, including us, is impermanent
- Nothing remains the same for two consecutive seconds
- Everything that is transient is unreal **KU4**

(b) *It is important to note that candidates are not required to write four different points in this answer. Credit should be given where candidates have expanded upon the points they have made.*

*Examples of areas covered:*
- Transience is caused by our avidya about the nature of the universe
- Transience leads to dukkha
- Transience leads to a misunderstanding of Brahman, atman and the jiva
- Transience is the cause of rebirth because we fail to see that each existence is part of maya **AE4**

(c) *It is important to note that candidates are not required to write four different points in this answer. Credit should be given where candidates have expanded upon the points they have made.*
*Examples of areas covered:*
- Path of action
- Can be atheistic
- Non attachment to fruits of actions
- Casteless
- Can be transferred easily between cultures
- Favoured by scholars as the most practical

- Does not require any ascetic behaviour
- Acts are done for the love of God **KU4**

(d) *It is important to note that candidates are not required to write eight different points in this answer. Credit should be given where candidates have expanded upon the points they have made.*

*Examples of areas covered:*

**Agree**
- Focus is on individual salvation
- Duty is essential and it could be at a social cost
- Might bring benefits but the motive is selfish
- It's about personal advancement so there is no true detachment
- Work of Gandhi
- Quick and obvious results at times

**Disagree**
- Strict ethical code which prevents selfishness
- Individual has to act rather than meditate so focus is on helping others
- Emphasises duty which helps society
- It is non political **AE8**

(e) *It is important to note that candidates are not required to write six different points in this answer. Credit should be given where candidates have expanded upon the points they have made.*
*Examples of areas covered:*
- Freedom from the cycle of rebirth
- Atman merges with Brahman
- Atman/jiva merges with Brahman
- Maya dissolves on attainment
- State of mind- cannot be described
- Bliss **KU6**

(f) *It is important to note that candidates are not required to write six different points in this answer. Credit should be given where candidates have expanded upon the points they have made.*
*Examples of areas covered:*
- It is personality
- Made up of a number of attributes
- It is who you are
- It is transient
- It is affected by karma
- It is afflicted by suffering and avidya
- It is part of maya **KU6**

(g) *It is important to note that candidates are not required to write eight different points in this answer. Credit should be given where candidates have expanded upon the points they have made. Candidates may score a maximum of four marks for one response. Candidates may take an approach other than agreement and disagreement with the statement. Examples of approaches:*

**Advaita**
- Jiva can be destroyed
- It is part of maya
- Atman uses jiva on its way to Moksha
- Jiva is mortal
- Jiva is transient and impermanent- can't escape to Moksha

**Visistadvaita**
- Jiva survives death
- Contributes to atman in its own distinctive way
- Jiva is real therefore can continue to live after death
- Only the body dies
- Jiva merges into Brahman with the atman **AE8**

# SECTION 4: Islam

(a) *It is important to note that candidates are not required to write four different points in this answer. Credit should be given where candidates have expanded upon the points they have made.*
*Examples of areas covered:*
- Comes in different forms: natural and moral

- Is a consequence of us misusing our freewill
- Is a test of Sabr
- Is part of life's test to see if we are worthy of Paradise or should be punished with Hell
- Part of the human condition
- Muslims believe Allah has a reason for everything. Therefore, suffering must be for a reason, even if it is not clear to us at the time. **KU4**

(b) *It is important to note that candidates are not required to write four different points in this answer. Credit should be given where candidates have expanded upon the points they have made.*
- **Allah – Creator.** He allows suffering to occur for a reason. It is part of His test for us.
- **Freewill.** When we misuse our freewill we cause suffering.
- **Khalifah.** He is testing us to see if we are good vice-regents. Do we help others to alleviate their suffering? Do we behave in a way that does not cause unnecessary suffering?
- **Risalah.** Through prophecy Allah has given us guidance on what is acceptable and what is unacceptable behaviour. We should know how to behave to cause minimum suffering.
- **Predestination.** Allah has planned the course of our lives. For everyone this will include moments of suffering and moments of joy.
- **Repentance.** Suffering can alert us to our wrongdoing and then motivate us to repent to Allah. **AE4**

(c) *It is important to note that candidates are not required to write four different points in this answer. Credit should be given where candidates have expanded upon the points they have made.*
*Examples of areas covered:*
- 2.5% of wealth to charity
- Means to purify or cleanse
- Duty
- Variety of collection methods
- Poor are exempt **KU4**

(d) *It is important to note that candidates are not required to write eight different points in this answer. Credit should be given where candidates have expanded upon the points they have made.*
*Examples of areas covered:*

**Agree**
- Money helps the poor, thus creates a more fair and equal society
- Sometimes the money is used to build new mosques, schools and libraries which benefits everyone
- It creates a more compassionate society
- It helps the Muslim community overcome jealousy and hatred

**Disagree**
- It helps the individual fight greed
- It helps them avoid making wealth and material possessions false gods (idolatry)
- It means they are submitting to the will of Allah so will be viewed favourably by Him
- If you are in a country where payment is voluntary it allows you to demonstrate sincerity
- Belief is put into action, shows how genuine your faith is **AE8**

(e) *It is important to note that candidates are not required to write six different points in this answer. Credit should be given where candidates have expanded upon the points they have made.*
*Examples of areas covered:*
- Live life in submission to the will of Allah
- Taqwa
- Ishan
- Examples of submission
- Follow teachings of Qur'an, Sunnah
- Follow Shariah law **KU6**

(f) *It is important to note that candidates are not required to write six different points in this answer. Credit should be given where candidates have expanded upon the points they have made. Examples of areas covered:*
- Flawed nature means we make mistakes
- Difficult to submit to Allah's will all the time
- Problems in the West – eg idolising money
- Shaytan may tempt
- Shariah harder to follow in non Muslim countries
- Difficulties of observing the Five Pillars
- Increased Islamophobia can make practice harder **KU6**

(g) *It is important to note that candidates are not required to write eight different points in this answer. Credit should be given where candidates have expanded upon the points they have made. Candidates may score a maximum of four marks for one response. Candidates may take an approach other than agreement and disagreement with the statement. Examples of approaches:*

**Significant**
- Gives meaning and purpose to life
- Reinforces belief of a just Allah
- Gives strength and comfort when times are bad
- Knowing we are being tested gives us the motivation to do good and avoid evil
- Good for society at large to make people accountable
- Reinforces Allah's omniscience

**Not significant**
- Other beliefs might be more significant
- Submission is more important because it determines afterlife
- Beliefs in Paradise/Hell because of inherent incentives
- Day of Judgement is problematic- life as a test could be seen as oppressive
- Confusing descriptions
- Paranoia – fear of being constantly judged **AE8**

## SECTION 5: Judaism

(a) *It is important to note that candidates are not required to write four different points in this answer. Credit should be given where candidates have expanded upon the points they have made. Examples of areas covered:*
- Free to choose
- Knowledge of good and evil
- Used freewill to disobey God in the Garden of Eden
- God sees the results of our choice but still allows us freewill **KU4**

(b) *It is important to note that candidates are not required to write four different points in this answer. Credit should be given where candidates have expanded upon the points they have made. Examples of areas covered:*
- evil and suffering can result from misuse of freewill
- disobedience leads to disharmony in relation to God and creation
- God's interaction with humanity influenced by use of freewill
- freewill affects balance between Yetzer Tov and Yetzer Harah but suffering can be inexplicable (eg Job) **AE4**

(c) *It is important to note that candidates are not required to write four different points in this answer. Credit should be given where candidates have expanded upon the points they have made.*

*Examples of areas covered:*
- Term can be used for entire Hebrew Bible and rabbinic teachings which followed or first five books of the Bible
- The word means 'Teaching'
- Its unifying concern is God's direction for the people of Israel
- Contains the 10 Commandments .... 613 Mitzvoth
- Talmud ... Midrash ... Mishnah ... Gemara

- On Mt Sinai both the written and the Oral Torah were given
- The Oral Torah is a detailed elaboration of the laws and beliefs contained in the written Torah
- It was formulated and transmitted in memory, handed on from prophets to sages, from masters to pupils, from the time of Moses. **KU4**

(d) *It is important to note that candidates are not required to write eight different points in this answer. Credit should be given where candidates have expanded upon the points they have made.*

*Examples of areas covered:*
**Agree**
- Depends on approach to Torah
- Literal interpretation could be very difficult
- Laws are very demanding
- Difficult to maintain traditions for thousands of years
- Difficult because social and historical changes should not affect the laws
- Reform/Orthodox views

**Disagree**
- Depends on approach to Torah
- Liberal interpretation makes them accessible
- Interpretations in Talmud make them more accessible
- Variation and adaptation permitted in some traditions
- Essence of laws is more important than the letter
- Reform/Orthodox views **AE8**

(e) *It is important to note that candidates are not required to write six different points in this answer. Credit should be given where candidates have expanded upon the points they have made. Examples of areas covered:*
- Obey God
- Live an ethical and just life
- Build a relationship with God
- Show obedience through keeping the laws
- Repent and forgive
- Work for a world of tolerance and peace
- Work towards creating the Messianic Age
- Be an example to the whole world **KU6**

(f) *It is important to note that candidates are not required to write six different points in this answer. Credit should be given where candidates have expanded upon the points they have made. Examples of areas covered:*
- The obligation to obey mitzvoth can be mechanical and restrictive
- Repentance is not an easy option
- Lack of understanding/empathy from non-Jews leading to prejudice and discrimination
- Problems associated with prayer, Tefillin, Mezuzah
- Practical problems in obeying the laws, eg access to kosher food, having to work on festival days etc
- Ethical issues, eg rights of the child in Brit Milah
- May feel as if life is just about following a set of rules
- Bound to the covenant for eternity **KU6**

(g) *It is important to note that candidates are not required to write eight different points in this answer. Credit should be given where candidates have expanded upon the points they have made. Candidates may score a maximum of four marks for one response. Candidates may take an approach other than agreement and disagreement with the statement. Examples of approaches:*
- Have made life hard at times eg Nazi Germany
- Have created suspicion in communities
- Have created isolation in communities
- Have set Jews up to be knocked down
- Have made it difficult for Jews to integrate
- Have brought the Jewish community together
- Have given security in an ancient and continuing tradition

- Have given Jews a clear role in society
- Have given Jews hope in times of despair
- Have helped in the fight against injustice
- Have united the world in the fight against discrimination and prejudice
- Have given the world an ethical code to live by- a code that exists to reduce suffering **AE8**

# SECTION 6: Sikhism

(a) *It is important to note that candidates are not required to write four different points in this answer. Credit should be given where candidates have expanded upon the points they have made.*
*Examples of areas covered:*
- God's order or Will
- Can only be known by studying the universe
- Can only be understood by the mind
- Means command
- Whole universe is under God's hukam **KU4**

(b) *It is important to note that candidates are not required to write four different points in this answer. Credit should be given where candidates have expanded upon the points they have made.*
*Examples of areas covered:*
- All life comes from God
- It is by following the Will of God that one can become one with God again
- Reunion with God cannot be achieved through mental effort alone, it is only by action, by living a life that is in obedience to God's Will (Hukam) that a person can make true progress towards reunion.
- Action is far more important than just knowing about God.
- It is also through God's Will that a Sikh may obtain God's Grace – it is through God's Grace that a person finally achieves reunion.
- However, Sikh's have a choice, free will as to whether they remain open to God's Grace and follow his Will or whether they choose to ignore God's Will and concentrate on material comforts or their own success.
- This would lead them to become stuck on the endless cycle of birth, death and rebirth.
- By following God's Will one can escape maya (illusion) **AE4**

(c) *It is important to note that candidates are not required to write four different points in this answer. Credit should be given where candidates have expanded upon the points they have made.*
*Examples of areas covered:*
- A religious congregation of Sikhs
- A source of guidance and inspiration in the daily lives of Sikhs.
- Spiritual progress is promoted through the sangat by attending congregational worship.
- Provides community support
- Provides spiritual support
- Meeting in the presence of the Guru Granth Sahib
- Used throughout Sikh history **KU4**

(d) *It is important to note that candidates are not required to write eight different points in this answer. Credit should be given where candidates have expanded upon the points they have made.*
*Examples of areas covered:*
**Agree**
- Important but not the only thing
- Moral principles of Sikhism
- Belief in God
- Sikh religious practices
- Other Sikh beliefs
- Spiritual importance
- Social importance
- Assists with spiritual quest
- Helps focus on God
- Educational benefits

**Disagree**
- Must be part of the community
- Community brings the individual closer to God
- Guru Nanak said Sikhs should be in the company of the holy
- Guru Granth Sahib is focus of sangat – should be there to learn from it **AE8**

(e) *It is important to note that candidates are not required to write six different points in this answer. Credit should be given where candidates have expanded upon the points they have made.*

*Examples of areas covered:*
- Goal of life
- Derived from jivan and muhkti- release life
- Attained the Ultimate whilst alive
- Escape of the soul from rebirth
- Freedom from the ego
- Gurmukh is one who has attained release
- Surrender to the will of God
- Liberation from human bondage **KU6**

(f) *It is important to note that candidates are not required to write six different points in this answer. Credit should be given where candidates have expanded upon the points they have made.*

*Examples of areas covered:*
**Sewa**
- Helping out in the Gurdwara
- Unpaid work in hospitals, old folks' homes etc
- Bring peace to people
- Help others with no ulterior motive
- Honest living
- Alert to serving others

**Simran**
- Repetition of God's name
- Sitting cross legged
- Meditation
- Calm the mind
- Concentrate
- Free yourself from attachment **KU6**

(g) *It is important to note that candidates are not required to write eight different points in this answer. Credit should be given where candidates have expanded upon the points they have made. Candidates may score a maximum of four marks for one response. Candidates may take an approach other than agreement and disagreement with the statement.*

*Examples of approaches:*
**Agree**
- Sewa involves taking action
- Living out the faith
- Setting a good example
- Faith is useless without practical action
- Simran is more self centred
- Jivan muhkti is a remote spiritual goal- sewa is happening in the here and now
**Disagree**
- Simran brings peace of mind and that can help society
- Common goal of Jivan Muhkti binds society
- Sewa is the result of Simran hence it brings benefits to all
- Sewa keeps the focus on God so actions undertaken are done so with God in mind **AE8**

# RM&PS HIGHER
# PAPER 1
# 2011

**Weighting of questions:**

*Knowledge and Understanding – approximately 50% of total marks available. The generic requirement for KU is that accurate, relevant and detailed knowledge of content is demonstrated; the information is presented in a coherent manner and information is communicated effectively using accurate terminology.*

*Analysis and Evaluation – approximately 50% of total marks available. The generic requirement for AE is for analysis of concepts, processes, evidence etc to be shown and evaluation to be balanced and informed.*

*No marks will be awarded where candidates simply provide a list. Any terms listed must be accompanied by a brief explanation to gain a mark. The bullet points under the heading of "suggested area covered in their answers" is a general guide as to the area that candidates may discuss in their answers. The examples are neither mandatory nor exhaustive.*

## SECTION 1

### Topic 1 – Crime and Punishment

1.  (a) *The issue addressed by the story must be stated.*

    *Suggested areas covered in answers:*
    - Source of morality
    - Are actions right in themselves?
    - Are actions right because God commands them?
    - Examples from the story
    - Implications of the issue
    - Examples from 'real life'.    **KU4**

    (b) *Each point about the Categorical Imperative should be accompanied by an explanation to gain a mark*

    *Suggested areas covered in answers:*
    - Moral absolute
    - Universal law
    - Examples can be used
    - Human reason can work it out from nature
    - One of the key principles alongside not using people as a means to an end and assuming the role of lawmaker.    **KU3**

    (c) *Each point about the source of religious morality should be accompanied by an explanation to gain a mark.*

    *Suggested areas covered in answers:*
    - Sacred writings
    - Human reason
    - Deity
    - Prophecy
    - Religious leaders.    **KU3**

    (d) *Candidates are not expected to write four separate points but may do so if they wish. As a general guide candidates may write 1-2 points with varying depths for each. Where new KU is introduced and used to make an AE point a mark should be awarded.*

    *Suggested areas covered in answers:*
    - Scriptural teaching on the issue
    - The teachings of religious tradition on the issue
    - The use of human reason on the issue
    - Views of religious groups on the issue.    **AE4**

2.  (a) *Suggested areas covered in answers:*
    - Who and where
    - What crime was
    - Info about crime
    - How CP was done/still on death row.    **KU3**

    (b) *Each example should be accompanied by an explanation to gain a mark. Candidates may write about one or more of the articles.*

    *Suggested areas covered in answers:*
    - Article 1: All human beings are born free and equal in dignity. This is denied by CP
    - Article 3: Everyone has the right to life. CP takes this away
    - Article 5: No one shall be subjected to torture or to cruel, inhuman or degrading treatment or punishment. By its nature, CP is all of these.    **KU3**

    (c) *A maximum of three marks for each reason. Candidates are at liberty to use either or both religious and secular criticisms of the viewpoint.*

    *Suggested areas covered in answers:*
    - All human life is special
    - Question of proof/certainty
    - Inhumane process
    - Brutalizes any society.    **AE6**

3.  (a) *Each point about community service should be accompanied by an explanation to gain a mark.*

    *Suggested areas covered in answers:*
    - Offender is sentenced to serve a community project
    - Set hours
    - Learn skills
    - Supervised at all times
    - Giving something to community.    **KU4**

    (b) *Candidates are not expected to write 10 separate points. As a general guide it is likely that candidates will write points with varying depths of explanation.*

    *Suggested areas covered in answers:*
    - Agreement with the statement
    - Disagreement with the statement
    - Implications of the statement
    - Positive impact of the statement
    - Negative impact of the statement
    - Moral issues surrounding the statement.    **AE10**

### Topic 2 – Gender

1.  (a) *The issue addressed by the story must be stated.*

    *Suggested areas covered in answers:*
    - Source of morality
    - Are actions right in themselves?
    - Are actions right because God commands them?
    - Examples from the story
    - Implications of the issue
    - Examples from 'real life'.    **KU4**

    (b) *Each point about the Categorical Imperative should be accompanied by an explanation to gain a mark*

    *Suggested areas covered in answers:*
    - Moral absolute
    - Universal law
    - Examples can be used
    - Human reason can work it out from nature
    - One of the key principles alongside not using people as a means to an end and assuming the role of lawmaker.    **KU3**

    (c) *Each point about the source of religious morality should be accompanied by an explanation to gain a mark.*

    *Suggested areas covered in answers:*
    - Sacred writings
    - Human reason
    - Traditions
    - Deity
    - Prophecy
    - Religious leaders.    **KU3**

(d) *As a general guide candidates may write 1-2 points with varying depth for each.*

*Suggested areas covered in answers:*
- Scriptural teaching on the issue
- The teachings of religious tradition on the issue
- The use of human reason on the issue
- Views of religious groups on the issue.　　**AE4**

2. (a) *Suggested areas covered in answers:*
- Lack of medical facilities
- Poor hygiene
- Infant mortality
- AIDs
- Lack of water
- Health problems arising from warfare
- Education
- Violence
- Health care.　　**KU3**

(b) *Each example should be accompanied by an explanation to gain a mark. Candidates may write about one or more situations.*

*Suggested areas covered in answers:*
- Lack of education generally
- Education targeted at boys
- Adult female illiteracy
- Lack of opportunities in work & careers
- Experience is beyond most
- Stereotyping – girls educated for domestic roles.　　**KU3**

(c) *Candidates are at liberty to use either or both religious and secular criticisms of the viewpoint.*

*Suggested areas covered in answers:*
- Domestic roles offer some protection to women
- Lack of employment in the developing world means that women have an important role
- Women keep the social network together
- Women are main source of educating children.　　**AE6**

3. (a) *Each point about changing roles should be accompanied by an explanation to gain a mark.*

*Suggested areas covered in answers:*
- More women in managerial positions
- Girls being educated equal or beyond boys
- Maternity no longer needs to result in career breaks
- Changes in law – equal pay & equal opportunities
- Changing expectations.　　**KU4**

(b) *Candidates are not expected to write 10 separate points. As a general guide it is likely that candidates will write points with varying depths of explanation. There is no limit to the number of responses that may be covered.*

*Suggested areas covered in answers:*
- Agreement with the statement
- Disagreement with the statement
- Implications of the statement
- Positive impact of the statement
- Negative impact of the statement
- Moral issues surrounding the statement.　　**AE10**

**Topic 3 – Global Issues**

1. (a) *The issue addressed by the story must be stated.*

*Suggested areas covered in answers:*
- Source of morality
- Are actions right in themselves?
- Are actions right because God commands them?
- Examples from the story
- Implications of the issue
- Examples from 'real life'.　　**KU4**

(b) *Each point about the Categorical Imperative should be accompanied by an explanation to gain a mark.*

*Suggested areas covered in answers:*
- Moral absolute
- Universal law
- Examples can be used
- Human reason can work it out from nature
- One of the key principles alongside not using people as a means to an end and assuming the role of lawmaker.　　**KU3**

(c) *Each point about the source of religious morality should be accompanied by an explanation to gain a mark.*

*Suggested areas covered in answers:*
- Sacred writings
- Human reason
- Deity
- Prophecy
- Religious leaders.　　**KU3**

(d) *Candidates are not expected to write four separate points but may do so it they wish. As a general guide candidates may write 1-2 points with varying depths for each.*

*Suggested areas covered in answers:*
- Scriptural teaching on the issue
- The teachings of religious tradition on the issue
- The use of human reason on the issue
- Views of religious groups on the issue.　　**AE4**

2. (a) *Suggested areas covered in answers:*
- CO2 emissions
- Deforestation
- Landfill pollution
- Reliance on fossil fuels
- Possibly part of natural cycle of earth.　　**KU3**

(b) *Each response should be accompanied by an explanation to gain a mark. Candidates may write about one or more responses.*

*Suggested areas covered in answers:*
- Kyoto
- Copenhagen 2009
- EU emissions targets
- Recycling schemes
- Global emissions targets
- International legislation
- The work of NGOs
- G8, 20 etc summits
- UN actions and policies.　　**KU3**

(c) *A maximum of three marks for each reason. Candidates are at liberty to use either or both religious and secular criticisms of the viewpoint.*

*Suggested areas covered in answers:*
- eg emissions targets are stringent
- Scientific evidence for GW is recent
- Still some doubt about GW
- Other pressing issues, eg poverty
- Uncertain if it is too late
- At least there has been a response.　　**AE6**

3. (a) *Each point about globalisation should be accompanied by an explanation to gain a mark.*

*Suggested areas covered in answers:*
- Global village
- Multinational corporations
- International banking & finance
- Media & communications
- Travel and mobility of population.　　**KU4**

(b) *Candidates are not expected to write 10 separate points. As a general guide it is likely that candidates will write points with varying depths of explanation.*

*Suggested areas covered in answers:*
- Agreement with the statement
- Disagreement with the statement
- Implications of this statement
- Positive impact of the statement
- Negative impact of the statement
- Moral issues surrounding the statement.    **AE10**

## Topic 4 – Medical Ethics

1. (a) *The issue addressed by the story must be stated.*

    *Suggested areas covered in answers:*
    - Source of morality
    - Are actions right in themselves?
    - Are actions right because God commands them?
    - Examples from the story
    - Implications of the issue
    - Examples from 'real life'.    **KU4**

    (b) *Each point about the Categorical Imperative should be accompanied by an explanation to gain a mark*

    *Suggested areas covered in answers:*
    - Moral absolute
    - Universal law
    - Examples can be used
    - Human reason can work it out from nature
    - One of the key principles alongside not using people as a means to an end and assuming the role of lawmaker.    **KU3**

    (c) *Each point about the source of religious morality should be accompanied by an explanation to gain a mark.*

    *Suggested areas covered in answers:*
    - Sacred writings
    - Human reason
    - Traditions
    - Deity
    - Prophecy
    - Religious leaders.    **KU3**

    (d) *Candidates are not expected to write four separate points but may do so it they wish. As a general guide candidates may write 1-2 points with varying depths for each.*

    *Suggested areas covered in answers:*
    - Scriptural teaching on the issue
    - The teachings of religious tradition on the issue
    - The use of human reason on the issue
    - Views of religious groups on the issue.    **AE4**

2. (a) *Suggested areas covered in answers:*
    - Illegal
    - England – assisted suicide illegal
    - Scotland – no suicide law, it is murder/culpable homicide
    - punishable by 14 years in prison.    **KU3**

    (b) *Each example should be accompanied by an explanation to gain a mark.*

    *Suggested areas covered in answers:*
    - Legal but only if strict criteria are met
    - Still a criminal offence if strict criteria are not met
    - Age limit
    - Medical procedure
    - Unbearable suffering
    - Persistent request
    - Legal, social and medical check ups
    - Alternatives explained.    **KU3**

(c) *A maximum of three marks for each reason. Candidates are at liberty to use either or both religious and secular criticisms of the viewpoint.*

*Suggested areas covered in answers:*
- UK laws don't protect from pain
- Euthanasia goes on in many forms so there is no protection
- Controversy over the use of the Liverpool Care Pathway (deep sedation and removal of nutrition) shows a lack of protection
- Inadequate end of life care
- Euthanasia cases regularly appear in court – stressful for all.    **AE6**

3. (a) *Each point about them should be accompanied by an explanation to gain a mark.*

    *Suggested areas covered in answers:*
    - Designer babies
    - Prevention of hereditary genetic conditions
    - Prevention of congenital conditions
    - Health issues with mother
    - Economic reasons
    - Eugenics.    **KU4**

    (b) *Candidates are not expected to write 10 separate points. As a general guide it is likely that candidates will write points with varying depths of explanation.*

    *Suggested areas covered in answers:*
    - Agreement with the statement
    - Disagreement with the statement
    - Implications of the statement
    - Positive impact of the statement
    - Negative impact of the statement
    - Moral issues surrounding the statement.    **AE10**

## Topic 5 – War and Peace

1. (a) *The issue addressed by the story must be stated.*

    *Suggested areas covered in answers:*
    - Source of morality
    - Are actions right in themselves?
    - Are actions right because God commands them?
    - Examples from the story
    - Implications of the issue
    - Examples from 'real life'.    **KU4**

    (b) *Each point about the Categorical Imperative should be accompanied by an explanation to gain a mark*

    *Suggested areas covered in answers:*
    - Moral absolute
    - Universal law
    - Examples can be used
    - Human reason can work it out from nature
    - One of the key principles alongside not using people as a means to an end and assuming the role of lawmaker.    **KU3**

    (c) *Each point about the source of religious morality should be accompanied by an explanation to gain a mark.*

    *Suggested areas covered in answers:*
    - Sacred writings
    - Human reason
    - Traditions
    - Deity
    - Prophecy
    - Religious leaders.    **KU3**

(d) *Candidates are not expected to write four separate points but may do so it they wish. As a general guide candidates may write 1-2 points with varying depths for each.*

*Suggested areas covered in answers:*
*A wide variety of answers is possible here. Candidates may refer to the following broad areas. Candidates may refer to any issue within the topic area identified:*
- Scriptural teaching on the issue
- The teachings of religious tradition on the issue
- The use of human reason on the issue
- Views of religious groups on the issue. **AE4**

2. (a) *Candidates may choose any weapon/treaty/accord they have studied.*

*Suggested areas covered in answers:*
- It is not banned by International Conventions
- It has ordinary ammunition and impact
- It is manageable and controllable in terms of its target
- It is used by most nations eg machine-guns, warships, grenades. **KU3**

(b) *Each example should be accompanied by an explanation to gain a mark.*

*Suggested areas covered in answers:*
- Weapons that are capable of a high order of destruction
- Nuclear weapons eg weapons that produce explosive energy through nuclear fission reactions alone, like atomic bombs
- Biological weapons. Weapons that use a living organism or natural poison to injure or kill, like anthrax
- Chemical weapons. WMD that use a poisonous chemical to injure or kill, like Sarin. **KU3**

(c) *A maximum of three marks for each reason. Candidates are at liberty to use either or both religious and secular criticisms of the viewpoint.*

*Suggested areas covered in answers:*
- World has been at war since 1945
- Deterrent has not stopped terrorism
- Race for deterrents cause insecurity
- Could precipitate war eg Iran, N. Korea
- Financial implications
- Potential loss of life
- Intent as bad as use
- Breach of international conventions. **AE6**

3. (a) *Each point about them should be accompanied by an explanation to gain a mark.*

*Suggested areas covered in answers:*
- No involvement in war at any level, even if you face jail
- No armed combat but assist in other ways eg help medical staff
- Express your views through campaigning eg lobbying MPs
- Petitions
- Marches. **KU4**

(b) *Candidates are not expected to write 10 separate points. As a general guide it is likely that candidates will write points with varying depths of explanation.*

*Suggested areas covered in answers:*
- Agreement with the statement
- Disagreement with the statement
- Implications of the statement
- Positive impact of the statement
- Negative impact of the statement
- Moral issues surrounding the statement. **AE10**

# SECTION 2

## Christianity: Belief & Science

1. (a) *Each point should be accompanied by an explanation to gain a mark.*

*Suggested areas covered in answers:*
- An argument for the existence of God or a creator based on perceived evidence of order, purpose, design, or direction, or some combination of these, in nature
- A priori argument
- Reasoning of Aquinas
- Reasoning of Paley
- Subsequent developments
- Use of analogies. **KU4**

(b) *Each point should be accompanied by an explanation to gain a mark.*

*Suggested areas covered in answers:*
- The changing seasons
- The lifestyle of animals and birds
- The intricate organisms of the human body and how it all fits and works together **KU4**

(c) *Candidates are not expected to write six separate points but may do so if they wish. As a general guide candidates may write 2-3 points with varying depths for each.*

*Suggested areas covered in answers:*
- Nature is chaotic
- Evolution
- The existence of suffering and evil
- The role of chance in nature
- The views of notable individuals
- The assumption of order in nature being imposed by cultural influences. **AE6**

2. (a) *No marks for simply stating that the cosmological argument is the first cause argument. Each point should be accompanied by an explanation to gain a mark.*

*Suggested areas covered in answers:*
- Causation
- Motion
- Contingency
- Change. **KU4**

(b) *As a general guide candidates may write 1-2 points of varying depths. Candidates may agree or disagree with the question.*

*Suggested areas covered in answers:*
- Big Bang suggests a beginning
- No pre-existing matter
- Something cannot come out of nothing
- Something had to cause Big Bang
- Big Bang is open to the same basic challenge as the existence of God – if nothing can come from nothing, who caused the Big Bang? **AE4**

3. (a) *Candidates must explain the terms used to gain a mark.*

*Suggested areas covered in answers:*
- A four stage process of…Observation, Hypothesis, Experiment, Verification
- Inductive and deductive reasoning
- Verification
- Falsifiable. **KU4**

(b) Candidates should provide either examples or explanations of different kinds of revelation to gain full marks.

*Suggested areas covered in answers:*

**General Revelation *'revelatio relis'***
• Nature.
• Reason.

**Special Revelation *'revelatio verbalis'***
• Bible.
• Jesus.
• Biblical figures.
• Miracles.                                            KU4

(c) Candidates are not required to write ten different points in this answer. As a general guide it is likely that candidates will write points with varying depths of explanation.

*Suggested areas covered in answers:*

**Agree**
*Scientific Method*
• Looks to understand the 'HOW' questions of the nature of reality
• Can provide data which can be independently tested by other scientists
• Has the capacity to change as new ideas, information become available.

*Religious Method*
• Many beliefs are not provable and more open to subjectivism, lack of evidence can be a problem. Who knows if it's really true?
• Humans can misinterpret experiences
• May see religious views as being superior to scientific ones.

**Disagree**
*Scientific Method*
• Cannot answer questions about meaning and purpose or values about how we should act or behave or on what basis
• Can give no idea of God
• Tends to approach reality in a reductive rather than a holistic manner so can be too narrow.

*Religious Method*
• Tends to deal with the WHY questions and the search for meaning, value and purpose in life
• Issues of faith go beyond the needs of science
• Looks for an overall 'big picture' which incorporates all aspects of the world and not just the scientific, observable ones – looks for ultimate causes and explanations
• Is more holistic and all embracing – especially at a philosophical level
• Deals with persons, beliefs, values etc which all have vital bearing on how we live.                        AE10

# RM&PS HIGHER PAPER 2 2011

*No marks will be awarded where candidates simply provide a list. Any terms listed must be accompanied by a brief explanation to gain a mark. The bullet points under the heading of "Examples of areas covered" are a general guide as to the areas that candidates may discuss in their answers. The examples are neither mandatory nor exhaustive.*

*NB Where candidates refer to appropriate sacred writings credit will be given. As a general guide a relevant and appropriate reference (which can be paraphrased or verbatim) will gain one mark. Where it is clearly applied to a concept of point it will receive a further mark. There is no limit on the number of references that can be used in an answer. However, relevance and appropriateness is essential.*

## SECTION 1: Buddhism

1. (a) *Each aspect should be accompanied by an explanation to gain a mark. Candidates may write about one or more of the articles.*

   *Examples of areas covered:*
   • Human condition is one of suffering – Dukkha
   • Suffering caused by not accepting anicca
   • Suffering caused by not accepting anatta
   • Attachment to impermanent things – tanha
   • 3 universal truths
   • Trapped on Samsara
   • Scriptures may be quoted.                    KU6

   (b) *Candidates are not expected to write six separate points but may do so if they wish. As a general guide candidates may write 2–3 points with varying depths for each.*

   *Examples of areas covered:*
   **Yes**
   • Not accepting anicca leads to craving and suffering
   • Craving permanence keeps you unenlightened and unenlightened actions lead to suffering
   • Unenlightenment leads to rebirth and to more suffering, so accepting anicca is basic to this.
   **No**
   • Other things also have to be accepted eg anatta
   • Attachment to self also leads to selfish actions
   • Selfish actions lead to suffering and rebirth so anatta also important.                                      AE6

2. (a) *It is important to note that candidates are not required to write six different points in this answer. Credit should be given where candidates have expanded upon the points they have made.*

   *Examples of areas covered:*
   • Can't be described, only experienced
   • Ultimate goal for Buddhists
   • 3rd Noble Truth
   • Unconditioned state of bliss
   • Not a place – not Buddhist heaven
   • Theravada and Mahayana interpretations.        KU6

   (b) *Candidates are not expected to write six separate points but may do so if they wish. As a general guide candidates may write 2–3 points with varying depths for each.*

   *Examples of areas covered:*
   • Ultimate goal for all sentient beings, so should be main focus
   • It is a very appealing goal, promising ultimate bliss so it is vital
   • If it wasn't there, no effort would be made to progress
   • It CAN be achieved

- Nibbana is too vague and inaccessible to have an impact
- Better to aim for better samsaric rebirth
- Unrealistic for lay Buddhists in Theravada. **AE6**

3. (a) *Each aspect should be accompanied by an explanation to gain a mark.*

*Examples of areas covered:*
- Abstain from killing
- Abstain from taking what is not given
- Abstain from sexual misconduct
- Abstain from false speech
- Abstain from intoxication. **KU4**

(b) *Each method should be accompanied by an explanation to gain a mark. Candidates may write about one or more ways of showing devotion.*

*Examples of areas covered:*
- Follow teachings
- Become monk
- Mark life cycle events with reference to him
- Forms of worship in Mahayana Buddhism
- Forms of recognition in Therevada Buddhism
- Art and literature
- Traditions and customs. **KU4**

(c) *It is important to note the candidates are not required to write eight different points in this answer. Credit should be given where candidates have expanded upon the points they have made. As a general guide candidates may write 3-4 points of varying depths.*

*Examples of areas covered:*
- Morality is an individual experience that is essential to gain enlightenment. Nobody can do it for you so Buddha is less important than own efforts
- Buddha can only show the way – devotion to him is not the main path; we have to keep our own morality
- Buddha discouraged excessive veneration paid to him personally
- True deep understanding of Dhamma and conduct resulting from that are superior to homage or emotional devotion
- Devotion
- The Five Precepts are the basic guidelines for Buddhist life which help to cultivate compassion, generosity. **AE8**

# SECTION 2: Christianity

1. (a) *Each aspect should be accompanied by an explanation to gain a mark. Candidates may write about one or more of the articles.*

*Examples of areas covered:*
- Gods relationship with human beings
- Created good
- Freewill/moral conscience
- Image of God
- Suffering and death
- Alienation through sin. **KU6**

(b) *Candidates are not expected to write six separate points but may do so if they wish. As a general guide candidates may write 2-3 points with varying depths for each.*

*Examples of areas covered:*

**Agree**
- Importance of the Fall
- Importance of God's promise of salvation
- Nature of humanity
- Link between sin and alienation
- Mission of Christ.

**Disagree**
- Depends on interpretation of scripture
- Moral message of Christ
- God's love rules over everything
- Universalist beliefs
- Role of Satan.
- Evaluation is balanced and informed. **AE6**

2. (a) *It is important to note that candidates are not required to write six different points in this answer. Credit should be given where candidates have expanded upon the points they have made.*

*Examples of areas covered:*
- Called to account for actions after death
- Result of disobedience
- God is just and applies his judgement to all
- Teachings of Jesus
- Links to the afterlife. **KU6**

(b) *Candidates are not expected to write six separate points but may do so if they wish. As a general guide candidates may write 2-3 points with varying depths for each.*

*Examples of areas covered:*
- Motivation to live a moral life
- Motivation to proselytize
- Motivation to seek salvation
- Love of God
- Follow example of Christ
- Take the sacraments. **AE6**

3. (a) *Each aspect should be accompanied by an explanation to gain a mark. Candidates may write about one or more tradition.*

*Examples of areas covered:*
- Roman Catholic eucharist
- Reformed practices
- Orthodox practice
- General descriptions also accepted. **KU4**

(b) *Each method should be accompanied by an explanation to gain a mark. Candidates may write about one or more ways of performing baptism. Maximum of two marks for one tradition.*

*Examples of areas covered:*
- Roman Catholic practice
- Reformed practice
- Orthodox practice
- Infant baptism
- Adult baptism. **KU4**

(c) *It is important to note that candidates are not required to write eight different points in this answer. Credit should be given where candidates have expanded upon the points they have made. As a general guide candidates may write 3-4 points of varying depths.*

*Examples of areas covered:*

**Communication**
- Brings community together
- Re-focus of faith
- Reminds community of what they are about
- Public witness of faith
- Can attract casual participants so spreads the net further.

**Baptism**
- Statement of belonging
- Statement of commitment
- Places obligations on people
- Part of an individual's identity
- Can attract non believers through presence of wider family at baptism. **AE8**

## SECTION 3: Hinduism

1. (a) *Each aspect should be accompanied by an explanation to gain a mark. Candidates may write about one or more of the articles.*

    *Examples of areas covered:*
    - Life is unsatisfactory because of suffering
    - Until a person overcomes suffering they will be constantly reborn, samsara
    - All life is a journey towards reunion with God
    - That Hindu's all are part of the all-pervading Brahman.   **KU6**

    (b) *Candidates are not expected to write six separate points but may do so if they wish. As a general guide candidates may write 2–3 points with varying depths for each.*

    *Examples of areas covered:*
    - By not understanding samsara – cycle of life a Hindu will get stuck on the wheel of life and fall into the trap of believing that this life is reality
    - However, it is not reality but rather an illusion – maya caused by ignorance – avidya
    - This creates additional problems for the Hindu in that the atman becomes captive in the material world
    - Importance of transience in the human condition
    - It could be argued that Karma is just important as samsara.   **AE6**

2. (a) *It is important to note that candidates are not required to write six different points in this answer. Credit should be given where candidates have expanded upon the points they have made.*

    *Examples of areas covered:*
    - It is material wealth
    - Artha includes the basic needs – food, money, clothing and shelter which allows people to have a comfortable home, raise a family, have a successful career and perform religious duties
    - Artha includes providing the personal and social means needed to enjoy kama, do dharma and attain moksha
    - Immoral actions, thoughts and intentions only lead to negative karma even if the result is a positive increase in wealth
    - By having wealth a Hindu can fulfil his ashrama dharma
    - Kama means desire
    - Involves relationship with others
    - Community involvement
    - One of the four purusartha
    - Lowest of the four purusarthas.   **KU6**

    (b) *Candidates are not expected to write six separate points but may do so if they wish. As a general guide candidates may write 2–3 points with carrying depths for each.*

    *Examples of areas covered:*

    **Artha**
    - Positive implications of artha is that it is a method of developing good karma as well as providing a way to fulfil dharma and attain moksha
    - Importance of wealth for carrying out duties
    - Artha is recognised as an acceptable personal goal as long as it is carried out according to Vedic morality
    - Not an end in itself but basic necessity, one must earn enough wealth in order to raise a family and maintain a household
    - Wealth must not be for hoarding but for sharing with those who are poor, handicapped or less fortunate kama
    - Balance of spiritual and material in life
    - Kama and karma yoga links
    - Guides and improves relationships
    - Could lead to materials.   **AE6**

3. (a) *Each aspect should be accompanied by an explanation to gain a mark. Candidates may write about one or more tradition.*

    *Examples of areas covered:*
    - Devotion to a deity
    - Daily devotion
    - Puja
    - Moral life.   **KU4**

    (b) *Each aspect should be accompanied by an explanation to gain a mark. Candidates may write about one or more tradition.*

    *Examples of areas covered:*
    - Ashramas
    - Dharma
    - Study
    - Life long.   **KU4**

    (c) *It is important to note that candidates are not required to write eight different points in this answer. Credit should be given where candidates have expanded the points they have made. As a general guide candidates may write 3-4 points of varying depths.*

    *Examples of areas covered:*

    **Jnana**
    - Dharma involves community in different ways
    - Expectations of making a contribution to the community
    - Responsibilities towards the community
    - Lifelong commitment to a goal gives stability.

    **Bhakti**
    - Brings community together
    - Moral life focuses on helping others
    - Focal point of the community
    - Maintains traditions and encourages acceptance and diversity.

    **Karma**
    - Community works for each other
    - Detached activity is better for all
    - No selfishness involved
    - Can be culturally transformed without difficulty.   **AE8**

## SECTION 4: Islam

1. (a) *Each aspect should be accompanied by an explanation to gain a mark. Candidates may write about one or more of the articles.*

    *Examples of areas covered:*
    - Humans are the apex of creation. Even placed above angels
    - Humans possess the gift of freewill
    - Responsibility comes with freewill
    - We are being tested by Allah on how we use or misuse it
    - Humans are guided by Fitrah
    - Aspects of life are predestined but we have freewill in how we respond to them.   **KU6**

    (b) *Candidates are not expected to write six separate points but may do so if they wish. As a general guide candidates may write 2–3 points with varying depths for each.*

    *Examples of areas covered:*

    **Agree**
    - It explains how we are the pinnacle of creation
    - It explains why there is suffering in the world
    - It explains our role as Khalifahs
    - It explains our special relationship with Allah.

    **Disagree**
    - Doesn't explain natural suffering
    - Understanding life is a test could be seen as more central.   **AE6**

**2.** (*a*) *It is important to note that candidates are not required to write six different points in this answer. Credit should be given where candidates have expanded upon the points they have made.*

*Examples of areas covered:*
- Muslims believe in a bodily resurrection
- Resurrected from Barzakh
- Resurrected in peak physical form
- Taken to Plain of Judgement to face Allah
- Three types: Minor, Middle and Great
- Resurrection is for everyone, not just Muslims.  **KU6**

(*b*) *Candidates are not expected to write six separate points but may do so if they wish. As a general guide candidates may write 2–3 points with varying depths for each.*

*Examples of areas covered:*
- No cremation
- Respect bodies more during life eg no drink or drugs
- Removes fear of death
- Gives hope, will meet loved ones again
- Reinforces other beliefs eg Allah is all-loving and all-powerful
- Motivates us to lead good lives and to submit to Allah.  **AE6**

**3.** (*a*) *Each aspect should be accompanied by an explanation to gain a mark.*

*Examples of areas covered:*
- Fast during the 29 days of Ramadan
- No food or drink between sunrise and sunset
- No wrongdoing or evil thoughts
- Muslims are excused if they are sick, under 12, pregnant, breastfeeding, old or travelling
- Those excused should provide food for the poor and needy instead.  **KU4**

(*b*) *Each aspect should be accompanied by an explanation to gain a mark.*

*Examples of areas covered:*
- Tawaf, circle the Ka'bah seven times
- Hurry between Marwah and Safa seven times
- Visit and drink from zamzam well
- Stand before Allah on the Mount of Mercy
- Stone Jamaras at Mina.  **KU4**

(*c*) *It is important to note that candidates are not required to write eight different points in this answer. Credit should be given where candidates have expanded upon the points they have made. As a general guide candidates may write 3–4 points of varying depths.*

*Examples of areas covered:*

**Sawm**
- Help them overcome elements of the human condition like selfishness and greed
- Develop empathy towards the poor
- Teaches the value of self-discipline and patience
- Healing quarrels by means if forgiveness.

**Hajj**
- Mount of Mercy: can be forgiven for all previous wrongdoing which will help secure a place in Paradise
- Climax of a Muslim's life
- Ihram reinforces equality before Allah
- A sense of brotherhood developed.

**Salat**
- Devotion to Allah
- Constant reminder of Allah
- Brings community together
- Most recognisable part of Muslim life.

**Ramadan**
- Discipline in the name of Allah
- Think about the poor
- Many take part in it
- Focus of community.

**Shahadah**
- Faith centres round this
- Everything is done to reinforce this belief
- Is at the centre of every religious and spiritual activity.  **AE8**

# SECTION 5: Judaism

**1.** (*a*) *Each aspect should be accompanied by an explanation to gain a mark.*

*Examples of areas covered:*
- Created in image of God
- God interacts with humanity throughout history
- Capable of living in harmony with God and creation
- Gift of freewill and its misuse
- Dual nature of humanity
- Suffering.  **KU6**

(*b*) *Candidates are not expected to write six separate points but may do so if they wish. As a general guide candidates may write 2–3 points with varying depths for each.*

*Examples of areas covered:*

**Agree**
- It emphasises human freedom and independence
- It allows us to understand the nature of God better
- It enables us to understand the dual nature of humanity
- Provides an understanding of where suffering and evil come from
- Allows an element of control over suffering and evil through choice.

**Disagree**
- Candidates may provide a variety of reasons why another aspect of the human condition is more important
- For example 'Image of God'…freewill can be seen as a part of this
- Everything that a Jew does is because he was created in the image of God.  **AE6**

**2.** (*a*) *It is important to note that candidates are not required to write six different points in this answer. Credit should be given where candidates have expanded upon the points they have made.*

*Examples of areas covered:*
- Common view that the Messianic Age will be a time of peace and harmony on earth.

**Orthodox**
- Messiah will be a man – prophet, teacher, leader
- Descendent of David
- Lead Jewish people back to land of Israel
- Will come either because the world is good enough – or too evil.

**Reform**
- Belief in Messianic Age is not mentioned in the Torah and so is a later introduction to Jewish belief
- They do not believe in coming of single person as Messiah, but teach about a future world in which human efforts will bring peace and harmony
- A time in the future where the spiritual bonding between Jews will bring about a world of harmony and a complete Jewish State
- All Jews are obligated to work towards this Messianic Age.  **KU6**

(b) *Candidates are not expected to write six separate points but may do so if they wish. As a general guide candidates may write 2-3 points with varying depths for each.*

*Examples of areas covered:*
- The 'standing out', the 'separateness' from others that all of many Jewish observances can bring, emphasises the Jewish identity of God's chosen people
- It defines and influences Jewish lifestyle
- To be an example to future generations
- Obligated to build a just and compassionate society throughout the world
- To cooperate with all men in the establishment of the kingdom of God, of universal brotherhood.　**AE6**

3. (a) *Each aspect should be accompanied by an explanation to gain a mark.*

*Examples of areas covered:*
- Torah rules
- Procedures for slaughtering
- Procedures for preparation
- Cooking procedures
- Organisation of the home
- The extent of leniency.　**KU4**

(b) *Each aspect should be accompanied by an explanation to gain a mark.*

*Examples of areas covered:*
- Start and finish times
- Friday procedures
- Shabbat services
- The Shabbat Meal
- The roles of different individuals
- The end of Shabbat.　**KU4**

(c) *It is important to note that candidates are not required to write eight different points in this answer. Credit should be given where candidates have expanded upon the points they have made. As a general guide candidates may write 3-4 points of varying depths.*

*Examples of areas covered:*

**Shabbat**
- Brings family together
- Brings community together
- Maintains identity
- Historically has helped maintain tradition.

**Kashrut**
- Keeps the community focused on their identity through an everyday activity
- Heightens awareness of faith
- Maintain identity
- Discipline.　**AE8**

# SECTION 6: Sikhism

1. (a) *Each aspect should be accompanied by an explanation to gain a mark.*

*Examples of areas covered:*
- One God who created everything and all creation is part of God
- Sikhs are on a journey to try to get back or reunite with God
- Human beings and all creation is an expression of God's Will (Hukam) and his divine spirit (Naam)
- All humans have an immortal soul (atman) and in order to reunite with God humans must do service to others (Sewa) and keep God at the forefront of their minds at all times (simran)

- Unfortunately it is not always easy to do this and people can get distracted from what is really important in life. These people focus on material comforts and wealth and move away from God's Will. They become haumai – self centred, egoism
- This also created Maya – illusion and this leads to negative Karma
- Negative Karma leads to a negative transmigration of the soul.　**KU6**

(b) *Candidates are not expected to write six separate points but may do so if they wish. As a general guide candidates may write 2–3 points with varying depths for each.*

*Examples of areas covered:*
- Agree to a certain extent, in that in order to remain true to the Will of God one must understand maya
- People are trapped in maya
- Maya leads to emotional attachment and love of duality and make a person forget God
- To achieve the goals of Sikhism one must overcome maya
- Maya is the cause of suffering.　**AE6**

2. (a) *Credit should be given where candidates have expanded upon the points they have made. A maximum of two per evil.*

*Examples of areas covered:*
- Kam
- Krodh
- Lobh
- Moh
- Ankar.　**KU6**

(b) *Candidates are not expected to write six separate points but may do so if they wish. As a general guide candidates may write 2–3 points with varying depths for each.*

*Examples of areas covered:*
- It leads the person away from reunion with God
- It makes a person haumai or manmukh
- A person cannot merge with God because they have turned away from God's Will
- A person will not be able to accomplish the other tasks in life such as sewa and simran, meditation, worship, study of the Guru Granth Sahib because they are too involved in their own pleasure to be able to focus properly
- The evils stop a Sikh from living a good life and being kind to others so they will not be able to achieve lasting happiness.　**AE6**

3. (a) *Each aspect should be accompanied by an explanation to gain a mark.*

*Examples of areas covered:*
- Remembrance of God
- Repeating the name of God
- Focus on God
- Reminds Sikhs of God's attributes
- Conquers ego, greed, attachment, lust etc.　**KU4**

(b) *Each aspect should be accompanied by an explanation to gain a mark.*

*Examples of areas covered:*
- Follow teachings of Nanak Dev
- Share wealth with others
- Give to charity
- Help anyone who does need it
- Be hospitable.　**KU4**

(c) *It is important to note that candidates are not required to write eight different points in this answer. Credit should be given where candidates have expanded upon the points they have made. As a general guide candidates may write 3–4 points of varying depths.*

*Examples of areas covered:*

**Nam Japna**
- Maintain Sikh identity
- Brings responsibilities to others with it
- Inspires people to act charitably
- Inspires people to spread the love and the word.

**Vand Chhakna**
- Clearly focussed on the community
- Brings material benefits to the disadvantaged
- Promotes equality
- Brings people together for a common goal.          **AE8**

## RM&PS HIGHER
## PAPER 1
## 2012

**Weighting of questions:**
*Knowledge and Understanding – approximately 50% of total marks available. The generic requirement for KU is that accurate, relevant and detailed knowledge of content is demonstrated; the information is presented in a coherent manner and information is communicated effectively using accurate terminology.*

*Analysis and Evaluation – approximately 50% of total marks available. The generic requirement for AE is for analysis of concepts, processes, evidence etc to be shown and evaluation to be balanced and informed.*

*No marks will be awarded where candidates simply provide a list. Any terms listed must be accompanied by a brief explanation to gain a mark. The bullet points under the heading of "suggested area covered in their answers" is a general guide as to the area that candidates may discuss in their answers. The examples are neither mandatory nor exhaustive.*

## SECTION 1

**Topic 1 – Crime and Punishment**

1. (a) *The issue addressed by the story must be stated.*

    *Suggested areas covered in answers:*
    - Is God the source of morality?
    - Is man the source of morality?
    - Is there a higher authority for morality than God?
    - Omnipotence of God
    - Does God act arbitrarily?          **KU4**

   (b) *No marks will be awarded for simply writing a list. Each point about Utilitarian Ethics should be accompanied by an explanation to gain a mark.*

    *Suggested areas covered in answers:*
    - Consequentialist ethical system
    - Actions are good if they have good consequences
    - Pleasure and pain
    - Based on the principle of the greatest good
    - Act Utilitarianism – principles applied to a particular situation
    - Rule Utilitarianism – principles applied as general rules based on past experience.          **KU4**

   (c) *A maximum of two marks per purpose of punishment will be awarded:*
    - Deterrence
    - Reformation
    - Retribution
    - Protection.          **KU4**

   (d) *Candidates are not expected to write four separate points but may do so if they wish. As a general guide candidates may write 1-2 points with varying depths for each. Where new KU is introduced and used to make an AE point a mark should be awarded.*

    *Suggested areas covered in answers:*
    - General good of society
    - Limiting crime for majority to lessen unhappiness
    - Increasing good through reformation
    - Families taken into account
    - Financial considerations.          **AE4**

2. (a) *No marks will be awarded for writing a list. It is possible for candidates to identify four points and where this is the case each point should be accompanied by an explanation. Candidates may illustrate their description by using examples.*

   *Suggested areas covered in answers:*
   - Stealing to survive/feed lifestyle
   - Depression – might turn to drugs
   - Poor education – unemployment – poverty – more crime
   - Poor housing areas – local criminal lifestyles.     **KU4**

   (b) *A maximum of three marks is available for each viewpoint. Where candidates write more than two viewpoints the best two should receive the marks. There is no requirement that the viewpoints should be conflicting or from different religions.*

   *Suggested areas covered in answers:*
   - Cycle of poverty
   - Society's attitude to poverty
   - Utilitarian concerns
   - Religious concerns
   - Kantian concerns.     **AE6**

3. (a) *Candidates are not required to write four different points nor are they expected to give more than one religious teaching. Candidates may, however, give examples of several religious teachings.*

   *Suggested areas covered in answers:*
   - The sanctity of life
   - The use of violence
   - Humans as agents of God's justice
   - Compassion
   - Teaching from tradition
   - Teaching from scripture.     **KU4**

   (b) *Candidates may refer to both religious and secular views on this statement. Candidates are not expected to write 10 separate points. As a general guide it is likely that candidates will write points with varying depths of explanation.*

   *Suggested areas covered in answers:*

   **Agree**
   - Religious statements on capital punishment
   - Religious support of offenders
   - Religious teachings on forgiveness
   - Religious teachings on retribution and justice
   - Sanctity of Life
   - Religion and human rights.

   **Disagree**
   - Not an issue that should concern religion
   - Ambiguous religious teachings on capital punishment
   - Cultural and moral development of the world.     **AE10**

## Topic 2 – Gender

1. (a) *The issue addressed by the story must be stated.*

   *Suggested areas covered in answers:*
   - Is God the source of morality?
   - Is man the source of morality?
   - Is there a higher authority for morality than God?
   - Omnipotence of God
   - Does God act arbitrarily?     **KU4**

   (b) *No marks will be awarded for simply writing a list. Each point about Utilitarian Ethics should be accompanied by an explanation to gain a mark.*

   *Suggested areas covered in answers:*
   - Consequentialist ethical system
   - Actions are good if they have good consequences
   - Pleasure and pain

- Based on the principle of the greatest good
- Act Utilitarianism – principles applied to a particular situation
- Rule Utilitarianism – principles applied as general rules based on past experience.     **KU4**

(c) *A maximum of two marks will be awarded per gender issue:*
   - Stereotyping
   - Roles
   - Equal Opportunities     **KU4**

(d) *Candidates are not expected to write four separate points but may do so if they wish. As a general guide candidates may write 1-2 points with varying depths for each.*

   *Suggested areas covered in answers:*
   - Issues and situations should be judged in terms of their possible outcomes
   - Principle of greatest happiness for greatest number should be applied (eg UK laws, equal opportunities at work)
   - Pain and unpleasantness should be avoided (eg sexism, denial of opportunities)
   - Application of Act/Rule Utilitarian principles depending on the situation.     **AE4**

2. (a) *No marks will be awarded for writing a list. It is possible for candidates to identify four points and where this is the case each point should be accompanied by an explanation. Candidates may illustrate their description by using examples.*

   *Suggested areas covered in answers:*
   - Human rights issue
   - Major activity of organised crime
   - Most trafficking involves females
   - Involves coercion and abduction
   - Slavery and sexual exploitation
   - UN protocols.     **KU4**

   (b) *A maximum of three marks is available for each viewpoint. Where candidates write more than two viewpoints the best two should receive the marks. There is no requirement that the viewpoints should be conflicting or from different religions.*

   *Suggested areas covered in answers:*
   - Lack of consent of the individual
   - Abuse and exploitation involved in sex trafficking
   - Discrimination against and unequal treatment of women and girls
   - Lack of respect for human rights
   - Religious concerns
   - Concerns arising from secular moral stances.     **AE6**

3. (a) *Candidates are not required to write four different points nor are they expected to give more than one religious teaching. Candidates may, however, give examples of several religious teachings.*

   *Suggested areas covered in answers:*
   - Equality of the sexes
   - Role of women
   - Justice
   - Teaching from tradition
   - Teaching from scripture.     **KU4**

   (b) *Candidates may refer to both religious and secular views on this statement. Candidates are not expected to write 10 separate points. As a general guide it is likely that candidates will write points with varying depths of explanation.*

   *Suggested areas covered in answers:*

   **Agree**
   - Created equal
   - Religious teachings on equality
   - Example of religious figures in dealings with women.

**Disagree**
- Goes against tradition
- Disrupts natural roles of males and females
- Religion is practically involved in empowering women
- Role of significant individuals.                    **AE10**

## Topic 3 – Global Issues

1. (a) *The issue addressed by the story must be stated.*

   *Suggested areas covered in answers:*
   - Is God the source of morality?
   - Is man the source of morality?
   - Is there a higher authority for morality than God?
   - Omnipotence of God
   - Does God act arbitrarily?                    **KU4**

   (b) *No marks will be awarded for simply writing a list. Each point about Utilitarian Ethics should be accompanied by an explanation to gain a mark.*

   *Suggested areas covered in answers:*
   - Consequentialist ethical system
   - Actions are good if they have good consequences
   - Pleasure and pain
   - Based on the principle of the greatest good
   - Act Utilitarianism – principles applied to a particular situation
   - Rule Utilitarianism – principles applied as general rules based on past experience.                    **KU4**

   (c) *A maximum of two marks will be awarded per cause.*
   - Pollution
   - Fossil fuels
   - Industrialisation
   - Failure to agree to protocols
   - Globalisation.                    **KU4**

   (d) *Candidates are not expected to write four separate points but may do so if they wish. As a general guide candidates may write 1-2 points with varying depths for each.*

   *Suggested areas covered in answers:*
   - Not current world population that will suffer
   - Life as a whole is what matters not just human life – all need to be protected from global warming issues
   - Pollution required to maintain levels of happiness with high standards of living
   - Fewer people directly affected by pollution than are affected
   - Application Act Utilitarian principles
   - Application of Rule Utilitarian principles.                    **AE4**

2. (a) *No marks will be awarded for writing a list. It is possible for candidates to identify four points and where this is the case each point should be accompanied by an explanation. Candidates may illustrate their description by using examples.*

   *Suggested areas covered in answers:*
   - Humans responsibility for stewardship of the environment
   - The teachings of religious traditions on stewardship
   - Practical actions and stewardship
   - Political actions and stewardship
   - Personal responsibility for stewardship.                    **KU4**

   (b) *A maximum of three marks will be awarded for each concern. Where more reasons are given then the best two should receive the marks. Candidates are at liberty to use either or both religious and secular moral concerns raised.*

   *Suggested areas covered in answers:*
   - Obligations to future generations
   - Ownership of the environment
   - Responsibility of all nations

- Obligations to other life on the planet
- Financial implications of effective stewardship
- Moral obligations placed on humans by God to care for the environment.                    **AE6**

3. (a) *Candidates are not required to write four different points nor are they expected to give more than one religious teaching. Candidates may, however, give examples of several religious teachings.*

   *Suggested areas covered in answers:*
   - Equality
   - Stewardship
   - Compassion
   - Teaching from tradition
   - Teaching from scripture.                    **KU4**

   (b) *Candidates may refer to both religious and secular views on this statement. Candidates are not expected to write 10 separate points. As a general guide it is likely that candidates will write points with varying depths of explanation.*

   *Suggested areas covered in answers:*

   **Agree**
   - Religious teaching on moral obligations to others
   - Religious teaching on equality
   - Practical response of religion to inequality.

   **Disagree**
   - Charity begins at home
   - Religion and capitalism
   - Religious teaching on poverty.                    **AE10**

## Topic 4 – Medical Ethics

1. (a) *The issue addressed by the story must be stated.*

   *Suggested areas covered in answers:*
   - Is God the source of morality?
   - Is man the source of morality?
   - Is there a higher authority for morality than God?
   - Omnipotence of God
   - Does God act arbitrarily?                    **KU4**

   (b) *No marks will be awarded for simply writing a list. Each point about Utilitarian Ethics should be accompanied by an explanation to gain a mark.*

   *Suggested areas covered in answers:*
   - Consequentialist ethical system
   - Actions are good if they have good consequences
   - Pleasure and pain
   - Based on the principle of the greatest good
   - Act Utilitarianism – principles applied to a particular situation
   - Rule Utilitarianism – principles applied as general rules based on past experience.                    **KU4**

   (c) *A maximum of two marks will be awarded per use.*
   - IVF
   - Research
   - PGD/PGS
   - Saviour Siblings
   - Stem cell research                    **KU4**

   (d) *Candidates are not expected to write four separate points but may do so if they wish. As a general guide candidates may write 1-2 points with varying depths for each.*

   *Suggested areas covered in answers:*
   - Application of The Greatest Happiness Principle
   - The embryo does not suffer
   - Stem cells are used to find cures for diseases
   - More pleasure created than pain?                    **AE4**

2. (a) *No marks will be awarded for writing a list. It is possible for candidates to identify four points and where this is the case each point should be accompanied by an explanation. Candidates may illustrate their description by using examples.*

   *Suggested areas covered in answers:*
   - Physician assisted death
   - Request from patient for assistance in dying
   - Easy/painless death
   - Applies to terminally ill or those with poor quality of life
   - Examples may be given. **KU4**

   (b) *A maximum of three marks will be awarded for each concern. Where more reasons are given then the best two should receive the marks. Candidates are at liberty to use either or both religious and secular moral concerns raised.*

   *Suggested areas covered in answers:*
   - The value of human life
   - Rights of the patient
   - Concern for medical staff administering euthanasia
   - Dignity of life
   - Quality -v- quantity. **AE6**

3. (a) *Candidates are not required to write four different points nor are they expected to give more than one religious teaching. Candidates may, however, give examples of several religious teachings.*

   *Suggested areas covered in answers:*
   - The sanctity of life
   - Definitions of life
   - Rights of embryo
   - Doctors' duties
   - Teaching from tradition
   - Teaching from scripture. **KU4**

   (b) *Candidates may refer to both religious and secular views on this statement. Candidates are not expected to write 10 separate points. As a general guide it is likely that candidates will write points with varying depths of explanation. There is no requirement that a balanced answer be given.*

   *Suggested areas covered in answers:*

   **Agree**
   - Human life is unique
   - Life is a gift from God
   - Scientists are 'playing God'
   - IVF used as a means for same sex couples to have children
   - Religious teachings can be given to support view.

   **Disagree**
   - Technology can relieve the suffering of infertility
   - Parents right to have a child
   - In an ever increasing secular world, religion is irrelevant
   - Moral duty to use technology to create life when nature fails
   - Free will/choice
   - Religious views can be given against IVF. **AE10**

## Topic 5 – War and Peace

1. (a) *The issue addressed by the story must be stated.*

   *Suggested areas covered in answers:*
   - Is God the source of morality?
   - Is man the source of morality?
   - Is there a higher authority for morality than God?
   - Omnipotence of God
   - Does God act arbitrarily? **KU4**

(b) *No marks will be awarded for simply writing a list. Each point about Utilitarian Ethics should be accompanied by an explanation to gain a mark.*

   *Suggested areas covered in answers:*
   - Consequentialist ethical system
   - Actions are good if they have good consequences
   - Pleasure and pain
   - Based on the principle of the greatest good
   - Act Utilitarianism – principles applied to a particular situation
   - Rule Utilitarianism – principles applied as general rules based on past experience. **KU4**

(c) *A maximum of two marks will be awarded per reason.*
   - Land
   - Resources
   - Pre-emptive strike
   - Historical reasons
   - Racism
   - Self-defence
   - Breach of treaties. **KU4**

(d) *Candidates are not expected to write four separate points but may do so if they wish. As a general guide candidates may write 1-2 points with varying depths for each.*

   *Suggested areas covered in answers:*
   - Launching an attack would be acceptable if it produces more happiness overall
   - The benefit gained from any response has to outweigh the pain caused by those who are killed, injured or bereaved in the process
   - Negotiation would be preferable as people on both sides would be happier if there is no bloodshed
   - Strengthening your defences would be appropriate as it may make your enemy back down, thus preventing the loss of lives and making a happier society. **AE4**

2. (a) *No marks will be awarded for writing a list. It is possible for candidates to identify four points and where this is the case each point should be accompanied by an explanation. Candidates may illustrate their description by using examples.*

   *Suggested areas covered in answers:*
   - Weapons that release biological agents when they explode
   - Weapons that use a living organism or natural poison to injure or kill
   - They aim to incapacitate or kill through the spread of disease
   - Explain examples like anthrax
   - They take out your enemies but leave the infrastructure intact. **KU4**

(b) *A maximum of three marks will be awarded for each concern. Where more reasons are given then the best two should receive the marks. Candidates are at liberty to use either or both religious and secular moral concerns raised.*

   *Suggested areas covered in answers:*
   - Inhumane
   - Indiscriminate
   - Not proportional
   - Not acceptable under the Geneva Conventions
   - Racial discrimination: nanotechnology being used to develop weapons that will target certain races
   - Damage to livestock and environment. **AE6**

3. (a) *Candidates are not required to write four different points nor are they expected to give more than one religious teaching. Candidates may, however, give examples of several religious teachings.*

*Suggested areas covered in answers:*
- The sanctity of life
- The use of violence
- The right to self defence
- Just War theories (from various religions)
- Teaching from tradition
- Teaching from scripture. **KU4**

(b) *Candidates may refer to both religious and secular views on this statement. Candidates are not expected to write 10 separate points. As a general guide it is likely that candidates will write points with varying depths of explanation.*

*Suggested areas covered in answers:*

**Disagree**
- Sacred texts' support of warfare
- Concerns of religious leaders/organisations on issues arising from war
- Just War Theories from different religious traditions
- Pacifism does not always lead to justice.

**Agree**
- Conflicting teachings in sacred texts on methods of war
- Conflicting messages from notable religious individuals or groups on the acceptability of killing
- Religious pacifism. **AE10**

# SECTION 2

## Christianity – Belief & Science

1. (a) *No marks will be awarded for simply listing or for simply stating General and Special revelation.*

*Suggested areas covered in answers:*
- God's way of communicating with Christians.
- Awareness of certain aspects of the world of nature
- Knowledge given to people by a divine/supernatural agent, eg God
- General Revelation - description
- Special Revelation - description
- Examples of General/Special Revelation. **KU6**

(b) *No marks will be awarded for simply listing. Each point should be accompanied by an explanation to gain a mark. Candidates are not expected to write four separate points. As a general guide candidates may write 1-2 points with varying depths for each.*

*Suggested areas covered in answers:*
- Depends on personal faith
- Not testable by observation
- Variety of interpretations
- Historicity is questioned
- Can be down to a matter of opinion. **AE4**

2. (a) *It is acceptable for candidates to describe the stages and/or to describe the nature of the Cosmological Argument.*

*Suggested areas covered in answers:*
- A posteriori argument
- Argument which claims to identify God as the first cause of the universe
- Argument from Causation
- Argument from Motion
- Argument from Contingency
- Argument from Change. **KU6**

(b) *It is important to note that candidates are not required to write six different points in this answer. Credit will be given where candidates have expanded upon the points they have made. As a general guide candidates may write 2-3 points with varying depths for each. Candidates may agree or disagree with the question. There is no requirement that a balanced answer be given.*

*Suggested areas covered in answers:*

**Agree**
- God could have caused the Big Bang.
- It is open to the same basic challenge as the existence of God – if nothing can come from nothing, who caused the Big Bang?
- Both give a complete picture of the Universe
- Big Bang suggests a beginning.

**Disagree**
- It provides an alternative 'first cause' to God.
- It is based on scientific evidence and not faith – it can be proved.
- Dealing with two different types of knowledge – how/why. **AE6**

3. (a) *No marks will be awarded for simply listing. Each point should be accompanied by an explanation to gain a mark.*

*Suggested areas covered in answers:*
- Survival of the fittest
- Random mutation
- Natural selection
- Small changes over time. **KU5**

(b) *Candidates may simply tell the story of Genesis 2. Where candidates confuse or combine the story with Genesis 1 no marks will be awarded.*

*Suggested areas covered in answers:*
- Adam created before Eve
- Created in the Garden of Eden
- No suitable partners
- Adam lonely
- Put Adam in a deep sleep
- Created Eve out of rib and dust
- Adam named Eve. **KU3**

(c) *It is important to note that candidates are not required to write ten different points in this answer. As a general guide it is likely that candidates will write points with varying depths of explanation. There is no minimum or maximum number of marks available for each point. Credit will be given where candidates have expanded upon the points they have made.*

*Suggested areas covered in answers:*
- 'Fixity of Species' -vs- 'Natural Selection'
- 'How' -vs- 'Why'.

**Agree**
- Creative process with God behind it
- Shows power of God and enhances belief
- Anthropic principle supports existence of an intelligent designer
- Acceptance by Christians that there is random chance but that the rules were formulated by God.

**Disagree**
- Does not see humans as different from other life forms
- The idea of God as creator seems to be left out if life developed in a natural way – no 'guiding hand'
- Meaning, Value and Purpose?
- Survival of the fittest seems to go against the idea of a loving God. **AE10**

# RM&PS HIGHER
# PAPER 2
# 2012

*No marks will be awarded where candidates simply provide a list. Any terms listed must be accompanied by a brief explanation to gain a mark. The bullet points under the heading of "Examples of areas covered" are a general guide as to the areas that candidates may discuss in their answers. The examples are neither mandatory nor exhaustive.*

*NB Where candidates refer to appropriate sacred writings credit will be given. As a general guide a relevant and appropriate reference (which can be paraphrased or verbatim) will gain one mark. Where it is clearly applied to a concept of point it will receive a further mark. There is no limit on the number of references that can be used in an answer. However, relevance and appropriateness is essential.*

## SECTION 1: Buddhism

1. (a) *No marks will be awarded for simply writing a list. Each aspect should be accompanied by an explanation to gain a mark.*

   *Suggested areas covered in answers:*
   - Actions
   - Unavoidable chain of cause and effect
   - Intention behind the act makes it good or bad
   - Good actions lead to good karmic payback
   - Fuels Samsara
   - Effects experienced later in this life or in next.      **KU6**

   (b) *A maximum of 2 marks will be awarded for each benefit.*

   *Suggested areas covered in answers:*
   - Heightens awareness of actions and how they affect others
   - Encourages control which leads to better karmic payback/rebirth
   - Helps them accept suffering and welcome it as a consequence of their own past actions
   - Spreads goodness into society
   - Control of three poisons.      **AE4**

   (c) *A maximum of 2 marks will be awarded for each difficulty.*

   *Suggested areas covered in answers:*
   - Life can seem unjust
   - Concern about constant responsibility for actions
   - Harder for laity
   - Negative belief.      **AE4**

2. (a) *No marks will be awarded for simply writing a list. Each aspect should be accompanied by an explanation to gain a mark. Candidates should write about two or more means to the goals of life.*

   *Suggested areas covered in answers:*
   - Buddha
   - Sangha
   - Dhamma
   - Eightfold Path.      **KU8**

   (b) *Candidates are not expected to write four separate points but may do so if they wish. As a general guide candidates may write 1-2 points with varying depths for each. Candidates need not agree about the importance and refer to other aspects of the faith as being more important.*

   *Suggested areas covered in answers:*
   - Brings balance
   - Eliminates 3 root poisons
   - Gives hope of rebirth and or Enlightenment
   - Helps eliminate causes of suffering
   - Buddha's teachings
   - Moral code contained in it
   - Path to Nibbana explained in it.      **AE4**

3. (a) *No marks will be awarded for simply writing a list. Each aspect should be accompanied by an explanation to gain a mark.*

   *Suggested areas covered in answers:*
   - No self
   - Nothing about us is permanent
   - 5 Skhandas
   - All beings inextricably bound together
   - Nothing passes on at rebirth
   - Reference to texts, eg Nagasena and the chariot.      **KU6**

   (b) *Candidates are not expected to write 10 separate points. As a general guide it is likely that candidates will write points with varying depths of explanation.*

   *Suggested areas covered in answers:*

   **Agree**
   - Not accepting anatta leads to craving and suffering
   - Attachment to false idea of permanent self keeps you unenlightened and unenlightened actions lead to suffering
   - Unenlightenment leads to rebirth and to more suffering, so accepting anatta is basic to this
   - Encourages selfless living so minimises suffering of all beings
   - Accepting anatta encourages awareness of the effect of the three poisons.

   **Disagree**
   - Other things also have to be accepted, eg anicca
   - Attachment to impermanent things also leads to selfish actions
   - Selfish actions lead to suffering and rebirth so anicca also important
   - Buddha as a role model is also important in understanding the human condition.      **AE8**

## SECTION 2: Christianity

1. (a) *No marks will be awarded for simply writing a list. Each aspect should be accompanied by an explanation to gain a mark.*

   *Suggested areas covered in answers:*
   - Dedication to God
   - Care for the sick
   - Love for enemies
   - Prayer
   - Parables
   - Baptism and communion
   - Resistance to temptation
   - Willingness to die.      **KU6**

   (b) *A maximum of 2 marks will be awarded for each benefit.*

   *Suggested areas covered in answers:*
   - Source of inspiration
   - Guide to live a moral life
   - Lead to salvation
   - Receive God's blessing
   - Participation in the sacraments
   - Source of strength in the face of persecution.      **AE4**

   (c) *Suggested areas covered in answers:*
   - Hard to live up to the standard set by Jesus
   - Loving enemies is major challenge
   - Resisting temptations of modern life
   - Challenges of living in a secular society
   - Different interpretations of scripture
   - Scepticism regarding the life of Jesus.      **AE4**

**2.** (a) *No marks will be awarded for simply writing a list. Each aspect should be accompanied by an explanation to gain a mark. Candidates should write about two or more means to the goals of life.*

*Suggested areas covered in answers:*
- Salvation
- The Resurrection
- The Sacraments
- Action against social injustice
- Kingdom of God.  **KU8**

(b) *Candidates are not expected to write four separate points but may do so if they wish. As a general guide candidates may write 1-2 points with varying depths for each. Candidates need not agree about the importance and refer to other aspects of the faith as being more important.*

*Suggested areas covered in answers:*
- Motivation to live a moral life
- Motivation to spread the 'good news'
- Means to eternal life
- Motivation to demonstrate love of God
- Follow example of Christ
- Involvement in the life of the Christian community
- Sins forgiven.  **AE4**

**3.** (a) *No marks will be awarded for simply writing a list. Each aspect should be accompanied by an explanation to gain a mark.*

*Suggested areas covered in answers:*
- Humans created in 'God's image'
- Freewill is central to human condition
- Moral conscience
- Freedom brings responsibility: disobedience to God's will has consequences
- Misuse of freewill results in sin and alienation
- The Fall.  **KU6**

(b) *Candidates are not expected to write 10 separate points. As a general guide it is likely that candidates will write points with varying depths of explanation.*

*Suggested areas covered in answers:*
- Without freewill sin would not have come into the world
- The Fall indicates that suffering is the result of humanity's free choice
- Alienation from God
- Alienation from nature
- Alienation from other people
- Sin can be overcome through salvation
- Christians use freewill to accept God's promise
- Without freewill love for God would not be real love
- Freewill builds a relationship with God
- Other aspects could be the key to understanding the human condition, eg the nature of God.  **AE8**

# SECTION 3: Hinduism

**1.** (a) *No marks will be awarded for simply writing a list. Each aspect should be accompanied by an explanation to gain a mark.*

*Suggested areas covered in answers:*
- Duty
- Eternal Law
- Universal Dharma
- Social Dharma
- Personal Dharma
- Linked to caste
- Linked to ashrama.  **KU6**

(b) *A maximum of 2 marks will be awarded for each benefit.*

*Suggested areas covered in answers:*
- Gives everyone a role
- Individual responsibility
- Community responsibility
- Social stability
- Respect for the environment
- Respect for others.  **AE4**

(c) *Suggested areas covered in answers:*
- Stifles ambition and personal development
- Strangles social progress
- Used to oppress
- Maintains the status quo.  **AE4**

**2.** (a) *No marks will be awarded for simply writing a list. Each aspect should be accompanied by an explanation to gain a mark. Candidates should write about two or more means to the goals of life.*

*Suggested areas covered in answers:*
- Sruti
- Swamis, rishis and gurus
- Ashrams
- Margas
- Detachment.  **KU8**

(b) *Candidates are not expected to write four separate points but may do so if they wish. As a general guide candidates may write 1-2 points with varying depths for each. Candidates need not agree about the importance and refer to other aspects of the faith as being more important.*

*Suggested areas covered in answers:*
- Less ego because it leads to suffering and illusion
- Detachment from illusion will allow the person to be open to spiritual and develop self-realisation
- Hindus have to remove themselves from the material concerns and not get caught up in the problems and suffering of everyday life
- This might make them appear to be selfish and uncaring.  **AE4**

**3.** (a) *No marks will be awarded for simply writing a list. Each aspect should be accompanied by an explanation to gain a mark.*

*Suggested areas covered in answers:*
- The atman is the 'divine spark' within humans
- It is permanent and changeless
- It is the same as Brahman
- Jiva
- Our aim in life is to realise that Brahman and atman are one
- In advaita our jiva is separate from the atman
- In visistadvaita our jiva has a presence in the atman.  **KU6**

(b) *Candidates are not expected to write 10 separate points. As a general guide it is likely that candidates will write points with varying depths of explanation.*

*Suggested areas covered in answers:*
- Karmic journey of the atman
- Understanding of suffering
- Understanding of Brahman
- Understanding of karma and samsara
- Avidya is the key
- Maya is the key
- Importance of the guru in understanding the atman
- Interpretations of advaita and visistadvaita.  **AE8**

## SECTION 4: Islam

1. (a) *No marks will be awarded for simply writing a list. Each aspect should be accompanied by an explanation to gain a mark.*

    *Suggested areas covered in answers:*
    - Eternal life starts when everyone is resurrected from Barzakh
    - On Judgement Day we will discover if we are to be sent to one of the seven layers of Paradise or one of the seven layers of Hell
    - Hell is a scorching place of torment, sorrow and remorse
    - People will wear chains and garments of fire
    - Paradise is a blissful abode for the righteous
    - Gardens with shade and flowing rivers. **KU6**

    (b) *Suggested areas covered in answers:*
    - Brings a sense of justice: the righteous will be rewarded and the sinful punished
    - Gives meaning and purpose to life
    - Motivates them to follow Allah's will
    - Gives comfort to the bereaved. **AE4**

    (c) *Suggested areas covered in answers:*
    - May be unnerved at the thought that angels are constantly recording our actions
    - May feel there are constraints on their freedom
    - It is unclear whether descriptions in the Qur'an should be taken literally or symbolically
    - The nature of Hell could challenge belief in a benevolent and forgiving Allah
    - Achieving a place in Paradise may seem unattainable, eg difficult following the five pillars and Shariah law in a non-Muslim country
    - Its true nature is beyond our understanding. **AE4**

2. (a) *No marks will be awarded for simply writing a list. Each aspect should be accompanied by an explanation to gain a mark. Candidates should write about two or more means to the goals of life.*

    *Suggested areas covered in answers:*
    - Live lives in submission to Allah
    - Taqwa and Ihsan
    - Repentance
    - Qur'an
    - Sunnah
    - Shariah
    - Five Pillars
    - Sadaquah. **KU8**

    (b) *Candidates are not expected to write four separate points but may do so if they wish. As a general guide candidates may write 1-2 points with varying depths for each. Candidates need not agree about the importance and refer to other aspects of the faith as being more important.*

    *Suggested areas covered in answers:*
    - Governs all areas of life: religious, social, economic and political
    - Motivates them to submit to Allah so they can gain entry into Paradise
    - Have to learn Arabic
    - Proves there is a God
    - Hearing it being recited led many to convert
    - Word of Allah therefore central
    - Central to those whose goal is hafiz. **AE4**

3. (a) *No marks will be awarded for simply writing a list. Each aspect should be accompanied by an explanation to gain a mark.*

    *Suggested areas covered in answers:*
    - Adam and Hawwah story
    - We can be disobedient because we have freewill
    - Misuse of freewill leads to suffering
    - We should repent when we have been disobedient
    - Allah has a reason for all suffering
    - We are not given more suffering than we can bear
    - Suffering is part of life's test. **KU6**

    (b) *Candidates are not expected to write 10 separate points. As a general guide it is likely that candidates will write points with varying depths of explanation.*

    *Suggested areas covered in answers:*
    - It explains why life is not perfect
    - It explains our flawed nature
    - It explains why humans do not remain equal
    - It highlights our weaknesses of greed and selfishness
    - Once these have been identified we can work at trying to overcome them and improve our lives
    - It explains what the problems are but not the causes
    - Need to understand the concept of freewill as well
    - Need to understand the nature and expectations of Allah
    - Need to understand our role as khalifah
    - Need to understand how to repent so we can gain Allah's forgiveness for being disobedient and causing suffering. **AE8**

## SECTION 5: Judaism

1. (a) *No marks will be awarded for simply writing a list. Each aspect should be accompanied by an explanation to gain a mark.*

    *Suggested areas covered in answers:*
    - Chosen People
    - Promise
    - Relationship
    - Freely entered into
    - Abraham/Moses
    - Circumcision/Ten Commandments
    - Symbols. **KU6**

    (b) *Suggested areas covered in answers:*
    - Reminds Jews they are still God's chosen people – special relationship
    - Gives a sense of identity – history/ancestors
    - Feel a part of something bigger than them – all Jews
    - Gives direction – should lead to living a moral life
    - Duty to be an example to the world. **AE4**

    (c) *A maximum of 2 marks will be awarded for each benefit or difficulty. Candidates must explain at least one benefit and one difficulty to gain full marks.*

    *Suggested areas covered in answers:*
    - Prejudice/Discrimination
    - Expectations of 21st Century life
    - Observance of mitzvoth requires dedication
    - Obey God in all things
    - Moral and social responsibilities. **AE4**

2. (a) *No marks will be awarded for simply writing a list. Each aspect should be accompanied by an explanation to gain a mark. Candidates should write about two or more means to the goals of life.*

    *Suggested areas covered in answers:*
    - Torah
    - Oral Traditions
    - Tzedakah

- Lashon Harah
- Shabbat
- Kashrut
- Bar/Bat Mitzvah.                                    **KU8**

(b) *Candidates are not expected to write four separate points but may do so if they wish. As a general guide candidates may write 1-2 points with varying depths for each. Candidates need not agree about the importance and refer to other aspects of the faith as being more important*

*Suggested areas covered in answers:*
- Part of moral and social responsibilities
- Helps achieve the goals
- Focus is on the treatment of one's neighbour
- Through loving your neighbour you show your love for God
- Important part of living a spiritual life
- By focusing on how you treat your neighbour you are keeping your Yetzer Harah in check.          **AE4**

3. (a) *No marks will be awarded for simply writing a list. Each aspect should be accompanied by an explanation to gain a mark.*

*Suggested areas covered in answers:*
- Yetzer Harah
- Instinct for survival
- Good when controlled – Evil when uncontrolled
- Tries to dominate our Yetzer Tov and make us lose this world and the world to come
- Yetzer Tov
- Moral conscience
- Good side of your personality/nature
- Exists within every aspect of Creation
- Suffering and evil in the world
- Human approach to God's will.                      **KU6**

(b) *Candidates are not expected to write 10 separate points. As a general guide it is likely that candidates will write points with varying depths of explanation.*

*Suggested areas covered in answers:*
- It explains why suffering exists in the first place
- Explains why Jewish people have suffered so much in the past
- Disobedience
- Dual Nature of Humanity
- Freewill
- Human responsibility leads to moral and social behaviour
- Suffering is often inexplicable – Job, Holocaust
- Consequence of Sin is further evil
- Torah study and observance aim to control the Yetzer Harah
- Allows an element of control over suffering and evil through choice.                                **AE8**

## SECTION 6: Sikhism

1. (a) *No marks will be awarded for simply writing a list. Each aspect should be accompanied by an explanation to gain a mark.*

*Suggested areas covered in answers:*
- A pure person
- Someone who is living a spiritual life
- Detached
- Obeying Gods Hukam
- Free from maya and haumai
- It is aim in life for a Sikh
- God – focused person.                              **KU6**

(b) *Suggested areas covered in answers:*
- It brings the person closer to reunion with God
- A person cannot merge with God without being Gurmukh
- Living in harmony with God's Will
- A person will be able to accomplish the other tasks in life such as sewa and simran, meditation, worship, study of the Guru Granth Sahib because they are not involved in their own pleasure and are able to focus properly
- Being Gurmukh means that a Sikh can avoid the pitfalls of maya – illusion
- Sikhs believe being Gurmukh makes you a better person as you are not distracted by anything.      **AE4**

(c) *Suggested areas covered in answers:*
- It may be that some think that being Gurmukh is selfish
- A person is thinking about their own goals and that may be considered to be individualistic and not necessarily for the good of the community
- The idea of leaving material possessions and not desiring anything may be a very difficult thing to do in today's society which is driven by wealth and possessions
- In order to sustain body and family one must work in order to get money to buy food and clothes. Being Gurmukh may be difficult to sustain with family and dependents
- It seems to contradict itself – to be spiritual and God centred but also to be part of the community
- Time to devote to being Gurmukh may be restricted in modern society.                               **AE4**

2. (a) *No marks will be awarded for simply writing a list. Each aspect should be accompanied by an explanation to gain a mark. Candidates should write about two or more means to the goals of life.*

*Suggested areas covered in answers:*
- Ten Gurus
- Guru Granth Sahib
- Equality
- Sikh spiritual path
- Kirt Karna
- Khalsa
- Sewa
- Simran.                                            **KU8**

(b) *Candidates are not expected to write four separate points but may do so if they wish. As a general guide candidates may write 1-2 points with varying depths for each. Candidates need not agree about the importance and refer to other aspects of the faith as being more important.*

*Suggested areas covered in answers:*
- Helps Sikhs to develop an understanding of Hukam
- Through its teaching the Granth enables a Sikh to lead a purposeful and rewarding life as a member of society
- Stresses peace and equality amongst people
- Offers guidance in all aspects of life
- They use this teaching in their daily lives, it is called Vak Loa which means "Taking advice"
- Helps Sikhs to become Gurmukh – focusing on God's word.                                             **AE4**

**3.** (a) *No marks will be awarded for simply writing a list. Each aspect should be accompanied by an explanation to gain a mark.*

*Suggested areas covered in answers:*
- Action – Law – actions have consequences
- Try to do positive karma and avoid negative
- Bad karma will affect the soul on its journey to reunion with God
- Bad karma will also affect the future rebirths of a person if they do not achieve reunion with God
- The law of karma is part of God's created order, not a force or power independent of God
- Karma is not the main focus in life for a Sikh – rather following the Will of God is more important.   **KU6**

(b) *Candidates are not expected to write 10 separate points. As a general guide it is likely that candidates will write points with varying depths of explanation.*

*Suggested areas covered in answers:*
- It may be considered to be very important because it is the way that Sikhs determine their actions
- By having to think about their actions it helps them to avoid bad or immoral behaviour
- It affects their next life which will affect their journey to God and ultimate reunion
- Positive karma helps Sikhs not to get bogged down by distractions, desires and material possessions
- A considered action keeps them in the real world and not suffering from maya
- Karma is not the most important thing in a Sikh's life – following the Will of God is more important
- A person who lives in harmony with the Will of God – Gurmukh, with God at the forefront of their minds no longer creates positive or negative Karma
- Humans as separated from God as a result of maya (ignorance) and haumai (egoism) – must recognise these in order to understand problems of human condition.
- Person's present condition is a result of karma, but liberation can only be achieved through an act of God's Grace.   **AE8**

## RM&PS HIGHER PAPER 1 2013

**Weighting of questions:**

*Knowledge and Understanding – approximately 50% of total marks available. The generic requirement for KU is that accurate, relevant and detailed knowledge of content is demonstrated; the information is presented in a coherent manner and information is communicated effectively using accurate terminology.*

*Analysis and Evaluation – approximately 50% of total marks available. The generic requirement for AE is for analysis of concepts, processes, evidence etc to be shown and evaluation to be balanced and informed.*

*No marks will be awarded where candidates simply provide a list. Any terms listed must be accompanied by a brief explanation to gain a mark. The bullet points under the heading of "suggested area covered in their answers" is a general guide as to the area that candidates may discuss in their answers. The examples are neither mandatory nor exhaustive.*

## SECTION 1

### Topic 1 – Crime and Punishment

**1.** (a) *Suggested areas covered in answers:*
- The second formulation of the Categorical Imperative
- A moral act will not use people as means to an end
- Treat people with dignity
- Don't exploit people.   **KU3**

(b) *No marks for simply writing a list. Each point about Utilitarian Ethics should be accompanied by an explanation to gain a mark.*

*Suggested areas covered in answers:*
- Based on the consequences of an action
- Based on the principles of pleasure and pain
- A moral act must aim to create the greatest happiness for the greatest number
- Act Utilitarianism considers the consequences of individual actions
- Rule Utilitarianism formulates general rules based on experience
- Historical development
- Examples can be given to highlight a point.   **KU4**

(c) *Candidate may illustrate their description by using examples and should be given credit for this.*

*Suggested areas covered in answers:*
- Criminal changes for the better
- Understands why crime was wrong
- Understands need to change
- Usually involves remorse/repentance
- Forms of reformation.   **KU3**

(d) *Candidates are not expected to write four separate points but may do so if they wish. As a general guide candidates may write 1-2 points with varying depths for each. Where new KU is introduced and used to make an AE point, a mark should be awarded.*

*Suggested areas covered in answers:*
- Deterrence can increase happiness if fewer crimes are committed
- The good achieved should be greater than evil done
- Reformation benefits all society if crime is not repeated
- Retribution acceptable if majority benefit
- Application act utilitarian principles
- Application of rule utilitarian principles.   **AE4**

2. (a) • Crime is caused by poverty
   • Crime is caused by social deprivation
   • Crime is caused by poor housing
   • Crime caused by economic pressures
   • Individuals commit crimes out of need rather than greed or desire
   • White collar crime can have an economic basis.   **KU4**

(b) *Candidates are not expected to write six different points although they should not be penalised if they do. There is no maximum or minimum number of marks for each point made.*

   *Suggested areas covered in answers:*
   • People know the difference between right and wrong
   • Criminal behaviour is a choice
   • Other people are poor and do not commit crime
   • Support for the poor is available
   • People try to live beyond their means
   • Poverty is not the cause – it is greed.   **AE6**

3. (a) *Responses need not be opposing responses nor do they need to be from different religions. Candidates must specify that the responses are religious and not simply opt for general moral responses to the issue. It is acceptable for candidates to use responses that might also be secular but an effort must be made to identify them as a religious point of view.*

   *Answers will probably cover issues from the general areas noted below:*
   • Interpretations of sacred writings
   • View of religious leaders
   • Practical action motivated by religion
   • Traditional teaching and practice.   **KU6**

(b) *It is important to note that candidates are not required to write ten different points in this answer. Credit should be given where candidates have expanded upon the points they have made.*

   *There is a significant range of responsibilities that can be covered so detailing all possibilities would be impossible. Answers will probably relate to the agreement or disagreement on issues arising from the general areas noted below:*
   • Interpretations of sacred writings
   • View of religious leaders
   • Practical action motivated by religion
   • Traditional teaching and practices.   **AE10**

**Topic 2 – Gender**

1. (a) *Suggested areas covered in answers:*
   • The second formulation of the Categorical Imperative
   • A moral act will not use people as means to an end
   • Treat people with dignity
   • Don't exploit people.   **KU3**

(b) *No marks for simply writing a list. Each point about Utilitarian Ethics should be accompanied by an explanation to gain a mark.*

   *Suggested areas covered in answers:*
   • Based on the consequences of an action
   • Based on the principles of pleasure and pain
   • A moral act must aim to create the greatest happiness for the greatest number
   • Act Utilitarianism considers the consequences of individual actions
   • Rule Utilitarianism formulates general rules based on experience
   • Historical development.   **KU4**

(c) • Monitor equality
   • Protect, enforce and promote equality across a wide range of areas
   • Provide support with issues arising from pregnancy and maternity
   • Raise awareness of equality and human rights issues.   **KU3**

(d) *Candidates are not expected to write four separate points but may do so if they wish. As a general guide candidates may write 1-2 points with varying depths for each. Where new KU is introduced and used to make an AE point, a mark should be awarded.*

   *Suggested areas covered in answers:*
   • Half the population are female so their happiness must be considered
   • Abuse, discrimination produce more pain than pleasure
   • Stereotyping (eg sexual) gives pleasure to many males – might outweigh the unhappiness of females
   • Rule Utilitarians might develop general rules based on equality and fairness
   • Application of act utilitarian principles
   • Application of rule utilitarian principles.   **AE4**

2. (a) *It is possible for candidates to identify four points and where this is the case each point should be accompanied by an explanation. Candidates may decide to describe fewer points in varying depths, but no maximum or minimum number of marks should be applied for each one. Candidates may illustrate their description by using examples.*

   *Suggested areas covered in answers:*
   • Giving women the skills and opportunities to make their own decisions
   • Access to education
   • Health rights
   • Voting rights
   • Financial independence
   • Freedom from oppression, exploitation and abuse.   **KU4**

(b) *Candidates are not expected to write six different points although they should not be penalised if they do. There is no maximum or minimum number of marks for each point made.*

   *Suggested areas covered in answers:*
   • Negative impact on men of unemployment
   • Emphasis on empowering women has had negative impact on men
   • Stereotyping of male roles puts unfair pressure on men
   • Negative impact on men of increased financial independence of women
   • Impact of feminist ideas
   • Diminished role of men in family and workplace.   **AE6**

3. (a) *Responses need not be opposing responses nor do they need to be from different religions. Candidates must specify that the responses are religious and not simply opt for general moral responses to the issue. It is acceptable for candidates to use responses that might also be secular but an effort must be made to identify them as a religious point of view. A maximum of three marks for each response.*

   *There is a significant range of responses that can be covered so detailing all possibilities would be impossible. Answers will probably cover issues from the general areas noted below:*
   • Interpretations of sacred writings
   • View of religious leaders
   • Practical action motivated by religion
   • Traditional teaching and practice.   **KU6**

(b) *It is important to note that candidates are not required to write ten different points in this answer. As a general guide it is likely that candidates will write points with varying depths of explanation. Credit should be given where candidates have expanded upon the points they have made.*

*There is a significant range of responses that can be covered so detailing all possibilities would be impossible. Answers will probably relate to the agreement or disagreement on issues arising from the general areas noted below:*
- Interpretations of sacred writings
- View of religious leaders
- Practical action motivated by religion
- Traditional teaching and practice.    **AE10**

## Topic 3 – Global Issues

1. (a) *Suggested areas covered in answers:*
   - The second formulation of the Categorical Imperative
   - A moral act will not use people as means to an end
   - Treat people with dignity
   - Don't exploit people.    **KU3**

   (b) *No marks for simply writing a list. Each point about Utilitarian Ethics should be accompanied by an explanation to gain a mark.*

   *Suggested areas covered in answers:*
   - Based on the consequences of an action
   - Based on the principles of pleasure and pain
   - A moral act must aim to create the greatest happiness for the greatest number
   - Act Utilitarianism considers the consequences of individual actions
   - Rule Utilitarianism formulates general rules based on experience
   - Historical development.    **KU4**

   (c) *Suggested areas covered in answers:*
   - Natural disasters
   - Trading inequalities
   - War
   - Politics.    **KU3**

   (d) *Candidates are not expected to write four separate points but may do so if they wish. As a general guide candidates may write 1-2 points with varying depths for each. Where new KU is introduced and used to make an AE point, a mark should be awarded.*

   *Suggested areas covered in answers:*
   - Increasing wealth does not provide commensurate increase in pleasure
   - Act in a way that will benefit many means that equal distribution could be an obligation
   - Minority benefits from unequal distribution so it is ethically wrong
   - Basic moral principle of equality bringing happiness to the greater number therefore we should act in a way that achieves this
   - Application of act utilitarian principles
   - Application of rule utilitarian principles.    **AE4**

2. (a) *It is possible for candidates to identify four points and where this is the case each point should be accompanied by an explanation. Candidates may illustrate their description by using examples.*

   *Suggested areas covered in answers:*
   - Emergency aid
   - Appropriate Aid
   - Tied Aid
   - Food Aid

- Technical Assistance
- Financial Aid.    **KU4**

(b) *Candidates are not expected to write six different points although they should not be penalised if they do. There is no maximum or minimum number of marks for each point made.*

*Suggested areas covered in answers:*
- Can help ensure that aid is used effectively
- Can help control corruption
- Can help restore or develop democracy
- Can remove a culture of dependency
- Can give access to valuable resources
- Can give strategic advantage to donor
- Can provide protection for population
- Can provide structure for chaotic states.    **AE6**

3. (a) *Responses need to be opposing responses nor do they need to be from different religions. Candidates must specify that the responses are religious and not simply opt for general moral responses to the issue. It is acceptable for candidates to use responses that might also be secular but an effort must be made to identify them as a religious point of view.*

   *There is a significant range of responses that can be covered so detailing all possibilities would be impossible. Answers will probably cover issues from the general areas noted below:*
   - Interpretations of sacred writings
   - View of religious leaders
   - Practical action motivated by religion
   - Traditional teaching and practice.    **KU6**

   (b) *It is important to note that candidates are not required to write ten different points in this answer. As a general guide it is likely that candidates will write points with varying depths of explanation. Credit should be given where candidates have expanded upon the points they have made.*

   *There is a significant range of responses that can be covered so detailing all possibilities would be impossible. Answers will probably relate to the agreement or disagreement on issues arising from the general areas noted below:*
   - Interpretations of sacred writings
   - View of religious leaders
   - Practical action motivated by religion
   - Traditional teaching and practice.    **AE10**

## Topic 4 – Medical Ethics

1. (a) *Suggested areas covered in answers:*
   - The second formulation of the Categorical Imperative
   - A moral act will not use people as means to an end
   - Treat people with dignity
   - Don't exploit people.    **KU3**

   (b) *No marks for simply writing a list. Each point about Utilitarian Ethics should be accompanied by an explanation to gain a mark.*

   *Suggested areas covered in answers:*
   - Based on the consequences of an action
   - Based on the principles of pleasure and pain
   - A moral act must aim to create the greatest happiness for the greatest number
   - Act Utilitarianism considers the consequences of individual actions
   - Rule Utilitarianism formulates general rules based on experience
   - Historical development.    **KU4**

   (c) • Patients with a terminal illness
   - No chance of recovery
   - Where there is unbearable and hopeless suffering

- Extremely poor quality of life
- Where all possible alternatives have been tried
- Where a living will has been made
- Specific case studies
- Forms of assisted suicide. **KU3**

(d) *Candidates are not expected to write four separate points but may do so if they wish. As a general guide candidates may write 1-2 points with varying depths for each. Where new KU is introduced and used to make an AE point a mark should be awarded.*

*Suggested areas covered in answers:*
- Application of The Greatest Happiness Principle
- Where no pleasure is produced, minimising pain is the focus
- Can reduce suffering for those involved
- Upholds the liberty of the patient's right to make choices
- Concern over non voluntary
- More pleasure created than pain?
- Application of act utilitarian principles
- Application of rule utilitarian principles. **AE4**

2. (a) *It is possible for candidates to identify four points and where this is the case each point should be accompanied by an explanation. Candidates may illustrate their description by using examples.*

*Suggested areas covered in answers:*
- Research into genetic diseases
- Research into causes of infertility, miscarriage
- Find cures/treatments/better drugs
- Better forms of contraception
- Process of creating stem cells
- Process of IVF. **KU4**

(b) *Candidates are not expected to write six different points although they should not be penalised if they do.*
- Question of personhood – embryos not sentient beings
- Only up to 14 days
- Can lead to cures to diseases
- Can lead to a reduction of generic disorders
- Can lead to improved drugs/treatments
- Offers hope for infertile couples
- Offers hope of a healthy child to couples who are genetically at risk
- Offers an opportunity to select desirable traits
- Can't undo scientific progress – duty to use this to improve human race
- Suffering of potential human beings is far outweighed by benefits to actual human beings. **AE6**

3. (a) *Responses need not be opposing responses nor do they need to be from different religions. Candidates must specify that the responses are religious and not simply opt for general moral responses to the issue. It is acceptable for candidates to use responses that might also be secular but an effort must be made to identify them as a religious point of view.*

*There is a significant range of responses that can be covered so detailing all possibilities would be impossible. Answers will probably cover issues from the general areas noted below:*
- Interpretations of sacred writings
- View of religious leaders
- Practical action motivated by religion
- Traditional teaching and practice. **KU6**

(b) *It is important to note that candidates are not required to write ten different points in this answer. As a general guide it is likely that candidates will write points with varying depths of explanation. Credit should be given where candidates have expanded upon the points they have made.*

*There is a significant range of responses that can be covered so detailing all possibilities would be impossible. Answers will probably relate to the agreement or disagreement on issues arising from the general areas noted below:*
- Interpretations of sacred writings
- View of religious leaders
- Practical action motivated by religion
- Traditional teaching and practice. **AE10**

**Topic 5 – War and Peace**

1. (a) *Suggested areas covered in answers:*
- The second formulation of the Categorical Imperative
- A moral act will not use people as means to an end
- Treat people with dignity
- Don't exploit people. **KU3**

(b) *Each point about Utilitarian Ethics should be accompanied by an explanation to gain a mark.*

*Suggested areas covered in answers:*
- Based on the consequences of an action
- Based on the principles of pleasure and pain
- A moral act must aim to create the greatest happiness for the greatest number
- Act Utilitarianism considers the consequences of individual actions
- Rule Utilitarianism formulates general rules based on experience
- Historical development. **KU4**

(c) • Negotiate
- Attack
- Strengthen borders
- Capitulate
- Turn to allies for support
- Impose sanctions
- Martial law. **KU3**

(d) *Candidates are not expected to write four separate points but may do so if they wish. As a general guide candidates may write 1–2 points with varying depths for each. Where new KU is introduced and used to make an AE point, a mark should be awarded.*

*Suggested areas covered in answers:*
- Benefits gained would have to outweigh the pain caused by those who would be killed, injured or bereaved in a conflict
- Negotiation would be seen as ideal because both sides would be happier if there is no bloodshed
- Strengthening your defences could act as a deterrent for aggressive nations, thus preventing the loss of lives and making a happier society
- Capitulating would be acceptable if it produces more happiness overall, you could put an end to the pain of your civilians and try and negotiate better conditions for them tied to your surrender
- Application of act utilitarian principles
- Application of rule utilitarian principles. **AE4**

2. (a) *It is possible for candidates to identify four points and where this is the case each point should be accompanied by an explanation. Candidates may illustrate their description by using examples.*

   *Suggested areas covered in answers:*
   - Weapons that use a poisonous chemical to injure or kill
   - Explain examples like Agent Orange, Sarin, Mustard Gas
   - They are more powerful than conventional weapons
   - May give examples of conflicts where they have been used. **KU4**

   (b) *Candidates are not expected to write six different points although they should not be penalised if they do.*

   *Suggested areas covered in answers:*
   - Possessed by others
   - Like for like strikes
   - Deterrent purposes
   - Can create panic
   - Can be indiscriminate thereby causing panic
   - Does not harm the infrastructure
   - Possession acts as a deterrent
   - They have been used successfully before. **AE5**

3. (a) *Responses need not be opposing responses nor do they need to be from different religions. Candidates must specify that the responses are religious and not simply opt for general moral responses to the issue. It is acceptable for candidates to use responses that might also be secular but an effort must be made to identify them as a religious point of view.*

   *There is a significant range of responses that can be covered so detailing all possibilities would be impossible. Answers will probably cover issues from the general areas noted below:*
   - Interpretations of sacred writings
   - View of religious leaders
   - Practical action motivated by religion
   - Traditional teaching and practice. **KU6**

   (b) *It is important to note that candidates are not required to write ten different points in this answer. As a general guide it is likely that candidates will write points with varying depths of explanation. Credit should be given where candidates have expanded upon the points they have made.*

   *Suggested areas covered in answers: There is a significant range of responses that can be covered so detailing all possibilities would be impossible. Answers will probably relate to the agreement or disagreement on issues arising from the general areas note below:*
   - Interpretations of sacred writings
   - View of religious leaders
   - Practical action motivated by religion
   - Traditional teaching and practice. **AE10**

## SECTION 2 – Christianity:  Belief and Science

1. (a) *No marks for simply writing a list. Suggested areas covered in answers:*
   - Observation, Hypothesis, Experiment, Verification
   - Induction
   - Deduction
   - Falsification
   - Models. **KU4**

   (b) *Suggested areas covered in answers:*
   - Cannot give us final/absolute truths or answer questions of meaning and purpose
   - Not all aspects of life can be known and understood by the processes of reason and the application of a systematic method
   - Because it is always changing, people may feel that it does not give us certainty in knowledge
   - Operates under certain assumptions which have to be taken as given – that the world is orderly, rational, and intelligible – cannot prove/show this to be the case. **AE4**

2. (a) *Suggested areas covered in answers:*
   - Explosion
   - Matter and anti-matter
   - Inflation
   - Formation of stars and galaxies, solar systems
   - Spontaneous natural event. **KU4**

   (b) *Suggested areas covered in answers:*
   - God could have caused the Big Bang
   - Both give a complete picture of the Universe – complimentary view not contradictory
   - Big Bang suggests a beginning just as Genesis does
   - Genesis does not attempt to be scientific
   - Accept scientific evidence. **KU4**

   (c) *Suggested areas covered in answers:*
   - The Biblical account has to be accepted as accurate
   - Science is provisional in its theories about origins
   - The scientific timescale does not match the evidence
   - Belief in what the Bible says is more important than scientific discoveries/evidence
   - Non-Overlapping Magesterium
   - Evidence used by science is a test of faith. **AE6**

3. (a) *Suggested areas covered in answers:*
   - Genesis 1
   - Genesis 2
   - Complexity of Human Body
   - Meaning and purpose in life
   - Bible is infallible word of God. **KU4**

   (b) *Candidates must refer to evidence/examples of evolution and not general principles to gain marks.*

   *Suggested areas covered in answers:*
   - Natural selection observed
   - Random mutation has been observed
   - Adaptation has been observed
   - Fossil record
   - DNA evidence
   - Missing link. **KU4**

   (c) *It is important to note that candidates are not required to write ten different points in this answer. As a general guide it is likely that candidates will write points with varying depths of explanation. Credit should be given where candidates have expanded upon the points they have made.*

   *Suggested areas covered in answers:*

   **Agree**
   - Creative process with God behind it
   - Shows power of God and enhances belief
   - Anthropic principle supports existence of an intelligent designer
   - Acceptance by Christians that the universe is governed by a combination of law and chance
   - Evolution may not be chance.

**Disagree**

- Common origin of life
- Natural selection/survival of the fittest
- It is a natural process which originated and developed in conjunction with the conditions on earth
- Human beings are not specially created but simply developed by a combination of chance and natural laws
- Human beings are not seen as unique but only the most advanced form of life on earth.  **AE10**

## RM&PS HIGHER PAPER 2 2013

*No marks will be awarded where candidates simply provide a list. Any terms listed must be accompanied by a brief explanation to gain a mark. The bullet points under the heading of "Examples of areas covered" are a general guide as to the areas that candidates may discuss in their answers. The examples are neither mandatory nor exhaustive.*

*NB Where candidates refer to appropriate sacred writings credit will be given. As a general guide a relevant and appropriate reference (which can be paraphrased or verbatim) will gain one mark. Where it is clearly applied to a concept of point it will receive a further mark. There is no limit on the number of references that can be used in an answer. However, relevance and appropriateness is essential.*

## SECTION 1: Buddhism

1.  (a) *Suggested areas to be covered in answers:*
    - Enlightened actions
    - Selfless actions
    - Compassionate acts
    - Actions that are free from greed, hatred and ignorance
    - Intentions and consequences.  **KU4**

    (b) *Suggested areas to be covered in answers:*
    - Mindful meditation clears the mind
    - Cultivates positive states of mind
    - Ends negative states of mind
    - Ends Tanha
    - Insightful meditation leads to enlightenment
    - Samatha/Vipasana
    - Loving kindness
    - Reference to Buddha's examples.  **KU4**

    (c) **Important**
    - It calms desires, so actions are not greedy
    - Gives insight to reality of no self so leads to selfless actions
    - Leads to control of mind, so all actions are considered
    - Leads to awareness of reality, so actions are enlightened
    - Leads to acceptance of anicca and anatta.

    **Not important**
    - Compassion is also necessary
    - Wisdom is also necessary
    - Discipline is necessary.  **AE4**

2.  (a) *Suggested areas to be covered in answers:*
    - Greed
    - Hatred
    - Ignorance.  **KU3**

    (b) *Suggested areas to be covered in answers:*
    - Constant round of rebirth
    - State of conditioned existence
    - State of unenlightenment
    - State of suffering.  **KU3**

    (c) *To gain full marks candidates must refer to at least one challenge for each concept. Candidates need not make a connection between the concepts to gain marks.*

    *Suggested areas to be covered in answers:*
    - Aim is to escape Samsara and end suffering
    - Won't achieve ending of Samsara while still possessing three poisons
    - Control of greed and attachments very difficult – survival of person
    - Letting go of ultimate attachment to self is extremely difficult
    - Must control the poisons in order to gain good Kamma to end Samsara.  **AE6**

3. (a) *Each aspect should be accompanied by an explanation to gain a mark.*

    *Suggested areas to be covered in answers:*
    • The teachings of the Buddha/Buddhist scriptures
    • The truth of Buddhism
    • One of the three jewels
    • Means to enlightenment
    • Theravada and Mahayana interpretations.            **KU6**

   (b) *Suggested areas to be covered in answers:*
    • Life today is still full of desires and attachments, so still a need for understanding of how to let go
    • Human condition still applies in modern world
    • Suffering still needs to be addressed
    • Three root poisons have greater hold in 21st century due to modern temptations so Dhamma may be even more relevant
    • Dhamma always there to be discovered for every lifetime
    • Universal truth
    • Constantly being revealed
    • Without dhamma there would be no point of the Buddha or Sangha
    • No point in meditation unless there was the dhamma to discover and follow.            **AE10**

# Section 2 – Christianity

1. (a) • Understanding his will
    • Understanding his nature
    • Allowing him into your life
    • Following the example of Jesus.            **KU4**

   (b) • Meeting of like minds
    • Worship
    • Prayer
    • Teaching
    • Social action.            **KU4**

   (c) **Important**
    • Reinforces faith
    • Presence of God at worship
    • Learning about God together
    • Visible commitment            **AE4**

   **Not Important**
    • Relationship is individual
    • Internal disputes
    • Denominational disagreements on doctrine and practice.

2. (a) • Alienation from God
    • Alienation from nature
    • Alienation from each other
    • Heaven/Hell
    • Judgement
    • Suffering.            **KU3**

   (b) • Loving
    • Omnipotent
    • Omniscient
    • Transcendent
    • Immanent
    • Creator
    • Sustainer
    • Personal.            **KU3**

(c) *To gain full marks candidates must refer to at least one challenge for each concept. Candidates need not make a connection between the concepts to gain marks.*

    *Suggested areas to be covered in answers:*

    **Sin**
    • Living a moral life
    • Self-denial
    • Repentance

    **God**
    • Meeting God's standards
    • Existence of suffering and evil
    • Contradiction between certain attributes.            **AE6**

3. (a) • Arrest
    • Trial of Jesus
    • Humiliation
    • Carrying the cross
    • The crucifixion
    • Words on the cross
    • Temple curtain.            **KU6**

   (b) *Suggested areas to be covered in answers:*
    • Suffering and death of Jesus was for all time and all people
    • Changes lives for the better
    • Inspires people to help others
    • Has created a more compassionate society
    • Human condition has not changed
    • Gives people hope of life after death
    • God has not superseded Jesus with anyone else.            **AE10**

# Section 3 - Hinduism

1. (a) • Final goal of life
    • Cannot be described, only experienced
    • Release from samsara cycle
    • Brahman and atman become one
    • Liberation.            **KU4**

   (b) • Positive, calm state of mind
    • Looks at the world objectively
    • No attachment to relationships, objects, etc
    • Dharma required in order to achieve detachment.            **KU4**

   (c) **Important**
    • Frees Hindu from attachment
    • Allows Hindus to understand that the self is not bound to the physical world
    • Key part of meditation
    • Necessary if following karma marga or jnana marga

   **Not Important**
    • Attaining moksha can be down to God's Grace
    • Bhakti marga has no requirement for detachment.            **AE4**

2. (a) • 'Illusion'
    • Mistaken attachment
    • Belief that material things are important/will bring lasting happiness
    • Fools humans into trusting impermanent reality.            **KU3**

   (b) • Means ignorance
    • Ignorance of the true nature of Brahman
    • Ignorance of the true nature of the self
    • Ignorance of the true nature of the universe
    • Ignorance of the cause of dukkha
    • Ignorance of the solution to dukkha.            **KU3**

(c) *To gain full marks candidates must refer to at least one challenge for each concept. Candidates need not make a connection between the concepts to gain marks.*

*Suggested areas to be covered in answers:*
- See the world as unreal
- Traps individuals in cycle of samsara
- Misunderstand your own nature – must try to understand the ego
- Misunderstand the universe – must try to recognise that everything is maya
- Must try to build good karma to overcome avidya.    **AE6**

3. (a) 
- Path of devotion
- The most popular marga
- Adoration of God in a particular form
- Active worship – participation
- Puja – offerings
- Moral life.    **KU6**

(b) *Suggested areas to be covered in answers:*
- No caste restrictions – open to all people
- Does not require learning/intellect
- Can be practiced anywhere, in any culture
- Practical in today's society
- Harnesses natural emotions
- Can be part of everyday life
- Does not involve self-sacrifice
- High moral code.    **AE10**

## Section 4 – Islam

1. (a) *Suggested areas to be covered in answers:*
- Green garden
- No extremes in temperature
- Flowing rivers and shade
- Cushions, carpets and thrones
- Silk robes and jewellery
- Milk and honey
- Seven layers.    **KU4**

(b) *Suggested areas covered in answers:*
- The Way of the Prophet
- It is the second most important source of guidance after the Qur'an
- The sayings and actions of Muhammad
- It helps Muslims deal with the practical problems that arise from living out the message of the Qur'an.    **KU4**

(c) *Suggested areas to be covered in answers:*

**Important**
- Muhammad is seen as the best example of how to live according to the Qur'an
- Gives the practical answers as to how you can achieve a place in Paradise
- Eternal truths contained in Sunnah

**Not Important**
- Necessary but secondary to following the Qur'an itself
- Qiyas and Ijma also needed to provide guidance on modern issues not covered in the Sunnah
- Observing the Five Pillars also necessary
- Using freewill wisely also necessary
- Repentance also necessary.    **AE4**

2. (a) *Suggested areas to be covered in answers:*
- Freewill
- Tested throughout our lives
- Pinnacle of creation, even above angels
- Allah's vice-regents (Khalifah)
- Unique.    **KU3**

(b) *Suggested areas to be covered in answers:*
- Al-Qadr, everything that exists or happens is an expression of Allah's will
- Everything is under His control, all has meaning and purpose
- Events in our lives happen as a result of Allah's will but we have freewill in how we react to these situations.    **KU3**

(c) *To gain full marks candidates must refer to at least one challenge for each concept. Candidates need not make a connection between the concepts to gain marks.*

*Suggested areas to be covered in answers:*
Predestination
- Have to trust Allah has a reason for everything, even when it is not clear what that would be
- Demonstrate Sabr
Uniqueness of humans
- Cannot lead a selfish life, have to use freewill wisely
- Can lead to a guilty conscience if we cause suffering due to misusing our freewill
- Have to repent, not always easy to admit you were wrong and have to make amends.    **AE6**

3. (a) *Suggested areas to be covered in answers:*
- Put everything else aside to fully concentrate on Allah
- Perform wudu
- Face direction of Mecca
- Rak'ahs
- Midday prayers on Friday performed in a mosque
- Set times (Fajr, Zuhr, Asr, Maghrib, Isha)
- If they are too ill to follow the physical steps they should still go through the motions in their hearts and minds.    **KU6**

(b) *Suggested areas to be covered in answers:*
- Even more important with the temptations and distractions of the modern world
- Performing it five times throughout the day at any point in history helps them live their lives as an act of submission
- These practices still teach them self-discipline and help them achieve Taqwa and Ihsan
- We have more hectic and busy lives in the modern world, Salah helps bring a sense of peace and tranquillity
- If they live in an non-Muslim country it is important they have a regular reminder and connection to Allah
- Also, in a mosque it will bring them together with others who share the same beliefs as them
- In any point in time training in cleanliness, purity and punctuality is beneficial
- In one of the Rak'ahs Muslims greet their two recording angels. This reminds them to repent for their wrongdoing. All humans whether in the past or present need to do this
- Muslims often perform Du'a prayers at the end. This allows them to feel better after asking for help or for repenting for their acts of wrongdoing.    **AE10**

## Section 5 – Judaism

1. (a) *Suggested areas to be covered in answers:*
- A time of peace and harmony for Jews on earth
- Will happen either because the world is good enough – or too evil
- Gathering in of Jews from all over the world
- Restoration of Temple
- End of sin and wickedness
- Orthodox/Reform views.    **KU4**

(b) *Suggested areas to be covered in answers:*
- Give relevant examples
- They mirror the split between the religious and ethical mitzvoth
- There are both positive and negative commandments
- There are commandments about outward actions and inner thoughts
- They cover relationships with God and other people. **KU4**

(c) *Suggested areas to be covered in answers:*

**Important**
- All Jews are obligated to work towards this Messianic Age
- Gives direction – should lead to living a moral life
- Duty to be an example to the world
- Reminds Jews they are still God's chosen people – special relationship
- Part of fulfilling the covenant

**Not Important**
- Other commandments equally important
- Other practices as important
- Belief and morality has moved on. **AE4**

2. (a) *Suggested areas to be covered in answers:*
- Caused by disobedience
- Caused by alienation
- Inevitable fact of life
- Caused by not following God's will/command. **KU3**

(b) *Suggested areas to be covered in answers:*
- Loving
- Omnipotent
- Omniscient
- Transcendent
- Immanent
- Creator
- Sustainer
- Personal. **KU3**

(c) *To gain full marks candidates must refer to at least one challenge for each concept. Candidates need not make a connection between the concepts to gain marks.*

*Suggested areas to be covered in answers:*
Suffering
- Historical suffering of Jews
- Unjustified suffering
- Purpose of the extent of suffering
God
- Meeting God's standards
- Existence of suffering and evil
- Contradiction between certain attributes. **AE6**

3. (a) *Suggested areas to be covered in answers:*
- Timing
- Preparations
- Synagogue service
- Observations
- Meal
- Role of each person
- Symbolism. **KU6**

(b) *Suggested areas to be covered in answers:*
- Continuity with the past
- Part of Jewish identity
- Strengthens family bonds
- Detachment from usual work routines
- Distinctive practice
- Focal point for the community
- Reinforces identity. **AE10**

# Section 6 – Sikhism

1. (a) • Freedom from rebirth
- Becomes one with God whilst still living
- Overcome maya and haumai
- No longer affected by karma. **KU4**

(b) • All human beings are equal
- Religious equality
- Social equality
- Gender equality. **KU4**

(c) • Keep God-focused
- Selfless-service
- Following example of Gurus
- Developing compassion
- Need an act of God's Grace. **AE4**

2. (a) • 'Illusion'
- Mistaken attachment
- Belief that material things are important/will bring lasting happiness. **KU3**

(b) • Self-centredness/egoism
- Motivated by thoughts of reward
- Even good actions are carried out to satisfy personal desires. **KU3**

(c) *To gain full marks candidates must refer to at least one challenge for each concept. Candidates need not make a connection between the concepts to gain marks.*

*Suggested areas to be covered in answers:*
- Have to recognise that God is only real and lasting part of creation
- Difficulty in avoiding attachment to family and friends
- Must recognise that true happiness cannot be found in material/worldly possessions
- Actions must not be motivated by personal gain
- Even good actions can be the result of desire to escape cycle of rebirth
- Religious practices can also be the result of haumai
- Maya and haumai are part of Hukam, so difficult to escape from. **AE6**

3. (a) • Outward signs of faith
- Follow teachings of Gurus
- No alcohol/tobacco/meat
- Reject caste
- Important role in community
- Set example to younger Sikhs. **KU6**

(b) *Suggested areas to be covered in answers:*
- Maintains tradition
- Provides role models to younger Sikhs
- Community profit
- Links to equality
- Seats of authority
- Resolve disputes
- Spiritual development
- Inner faith forums. **AE10**